# HEARTFELT
# MARKETING

# HEARTFELT MARKETING

*Allowing the Universe*

*to Be Your Business Partner*

## Jacquie Jordan

**BURMAN**BOOKS
.COM

HEARTFELT MARKETING

Copyright © 2010 by Jacquie Jordan

Published by
BurmanBooks Entertainment
A Road A Head Films
260 Queens Quay West, Suite 1102
Toronto, Ontario M5J 2N3

Interior book design by Barbara Aronica-Buck

Book cover designed by Jonathan Fong

ISBN 9781897404270

www.tvguestpert.com

First Printing December 2010
Printed in the United States of America
10 9 8 7 6 5 4 3 2 1

*To Richard Waner*

*Every woman deserves a champion.*

*Thank you for being mine.*

# CONTENTS

# ACKNOWLEDGEMENTS

I have been privileged to work with many gifted people. New folks are showing up every day and offering me new and exciting perspectives on my life and my business. Then there are those whom I've been working with over time and who were directly involved in the making of this book. I am in deep gratitude for their generosity and wisdom. Here is a partial list of them and some of their contributions:

Chris McLean, for holding the vision for the workshop and its content back when it was called "Spiritual Marketing," before it was thought that this name could be a religious statement. Amy Superfood Fairy and Patrick Smith, for the faith. Sharon and Jeff, for the practice of heartfelt friendship.

Darice Fisher, for being absolutely solid. (Darice, remember that night when we said, "Why can't we find the twenty-year-old versions of us?") Stephanie Cobian, for being the best assistant ever!

Starla & Kriz, for always making me look good – the cover captures the essence. Jordan, for the patience and talent you showed in bringing out my concept for the cover. Jonathan, for taking Chris' idea and yours and merging the two to create the concept that, in spite of day-to-day insanity and chaos, we can still live from our hearts.

All the Guestperts™ – the most amazing messengers of Heartfelt Messages.

The Burman Books gang: Sanjay Burman and John Manikaros, for their faithful support. Barbara Aronica, for her patience with the endless back-and-forth of changes in details. For the ghost team – Mark Parsons, Stephen Hornyak and Lanie Adamson and team for editing the first draft manuscript.

# INTRODUCTION

The intention of this book is to share with you my definition of success and, based on that definition, share ways of applying it to your business and making a contribution to others. You may or may not agree with me. The best possible scenario is that you will develop your own definition of success and not allow others to do that for you. I've had a lot of professional "success" during my time as a television producer – Emmy® nominations, money, prestige, and elbow-rubbing with the rich and famous.

My definition of success is quite different today. I suspect, given the recent changes in the global economy, that I am not alone. What you might expect me to write next is the following cliché: "I have less money and fewer things now, but I am successful, because I am far happier than I was when I had all that stuff." That actually is not my truth either as that does not define my version of success. We must define our own version of success.

However, it is important for us to anchor ourselves in our own reality and our own purpose and to take care of ourselves, our responsibilities, and our obligations fully to the best of our ability on a daily basis.

1. So that we are not drawn into the big fear, the tornado or quicksand of drama.

2. That we can bring forward what we have here, which is our experience, strength and hope and we do that through the assets of our goals and our service to others.

My hope with you on the journey with me through this book is to synch up your internal beliefs about who you are, what you are trying to create, why you are trying to do it, and how you can be of service through the expression of your vocation or your business through the busy-ness of daily living.

I come from working in the talk-television industry, a highly pressured and competitive arena. Out of my television career grew the media development business that I own today, where I can offer my professional input and experience by helping others with their own career trajectories. I've experienced success, and I've also experienced the ground beneath my feet suddenly shifting and dropping away. That's a scary place to be! But I learned many valuable lessons along the way, and that's why I wrote Heartfelt Marketing – to share my experience and show you how to thrive, survive, prosper and enjoy life in the professional marketplace, coming from your heart, not your head.

# AUTHOR'S NOTE

I had the opportunity to publish my book this month. I was behind. I wanted it to be between 40,000 and 60,000 words, but I was at 20,000 words. It was supposed to be a hard-cover book, and it was becoming a soft–cover. Three of my Big Name celebrity endorsements had backed out, for one polite reason or another. My clients' projects always seemed to take precedence over my own deadlines and deliverables. The direction of what I was teaching in workshops was not coming out on paper. In fact, I felt like I was writing an entirely different book.

Six weeks ago, I got a gentle call from my publisher. "Jacquie, how's the book coming?" In my head, I answered, "It's not." Out of my mouth came, "It's good. Can't wait for you to have it."

Panic. Panic. Panic. Perfectionism. Perfectionism. Perfectionism.

I wanted to call him back and renegotiate. "Can we deliver in the next quarter?"

But the truth always *Is* – if not now, when? Were my circumstances, responsibilities, workload, commitments, going to change? Was a bestseller going to come out of me in three more months? Should I really be kneading the bread any longer?

And this is how the dance goes.

I then realized that my clients have been my greatest teachers. I have witnessed, over and over again, the presentation of opportunity and the reaction of many folks (not all), as they push back on the door they so wanted opened.

I realized that getting this book completed was simply not going to be comfortable. I quickly accepted the realization that it might not be more than 20,000 words, reducing the size from the outline's projection of 225 pages to 90 pages. I also realized that this book might not be my bestseller, after all.

What I did *own,* in the moment, was that I was (and am) not going to desert myself and bow to perfectionism. That it doesn't have to be perfect. That this may be my second book of 32 books. How was I to know? The bottom line is – Show *up!*

Which means that I risk being judged, criticized, not famous, and not wealthy because of this book. It also means that I am standing by this book as an offering. I am saying: This is who I am. This is what I've learned. I choose to risk coming from the heart, not from the head, to share with you what I know.

So please accept my humble writings, as I put into motion what I am practicing – which is living and doing business from a place of authenticity. Taking the risk of putting myself out there is the essence of Heartfelt Marketing because I believe I have something to offer that would be of service.

# CHAPTER 1

# The World Out of Balance

Collectively, we're in pretty tough shape. It is clear that the way the world has been run is not self-supporting. We're overdrawn. We're overextended. What used to work no longer works. *En masse,* we are experiencing a kind of collective Spiritual Bankruptcy.

But those of us reading this book don't need to be part of that treacherous collective. We don't need to get swept up in other people's terrors or breakdowns, and we don't need to go down with the ship. Just because you, or someone you know, is having an external breakdown, that's not necessarily a bad thing. Oftentimes a breakdown leads to a breakthrough. Outside the intense discomfort of the unknown and the projection of catastrophic, worst-case scenarios, the "breakdowns" actually create space or room for new, creative life-growth and solutions to enter. Sometimes we have to let go of the old to make room for the new.

Before we explore those solutions in Heartfelt Marketing, let's take off the gloves and get honest about how we got where we are.

We are out of balance due to spiritual and material bankruptcy. When I use the term spiritual bankruptcy, or bankruptcy of the heart, I mean a state of imbalance in which we are not connected to our hearts or our souls. In this state, we focus on the material, and we lose sight of who we are and why we are here.

Its opposite kissing cousin is material bankruptcy, in which we lose our homes, businesses, credit ratings – when all *seems* lost. The two states of mind are polar opposites, yet they feed off each other and make us fearful. Fear feeds fear in a vicious cycle. It is a trap, but a trap from which we can escape.

Spiritual bankruptcy comes when we value material things more than our hearts, either consciously or unconsciously. Either way, we are alienated from the best we have to offer: ourselves, our hearts, and our souls. In this state, we are also alienated from the talents and skills that we can use to become satisfied, rightfully rewarded contributors to society. These talents and skill are our gifts. Each one of us can use them to leave our life's thumbprint.

When we have money fear, career malaise or financial panic, we start to lose ourselves, and our focus becomes solely material. When the material aspects of life are all that we can see and all that we can think about, we slip into a downward spiral. But we can step off of this downward spiral. This book is about getting into a state of complementary harmony between our interior state of being (heart and spirit) and our exterior state of being (our careers and businesses, or day-to-day busy-nesses). And achieving that balance is all about listening to stories and advice, like the material in this book, and applying them to our lives.

You can start this process now. In fact, you already have, by reading these words. And while learning how to balance takes some time, once we have it, it becomes second nature. When we learn to ride a bike, we wobble and fall and skin our knees, but once we master the skill, we never forget it. We ride on confidently and get where we are going.

The balance, the integration, the complementary harmony that each of us is looking for is the ability to make a living by following our heart's desire. It's simple, but it's not easy. Otherwise most folks would be able to answer in the affirmative if we asked them if they are living their dreams. When we are living our dreams (and *by the act of* living our dreams), we are fully self-supporting – we are in spiritual and material integration.

# CHAPTER 2

# The Beginning of Balance

## RELEASING AND ALLOWING

Releasing, releasing, releasing. Allowing, allowing, allowing. Remember the old real estate adage, "Location, location, location?" Here in Heartfelt Marketing, *Allowing,* and its sibling *Releasing,* will be the basic tools in your kit. You will learn to:

- Release blocks that are getting in the way of business expansion.

- Release "energetic tackiness" that screams inferiority in your business exchanges.

- Release the Five Pitfalls that spell doom to revenue generation.

- Allow yourself to see that intention and language make a *huge* difference in the sale.

- Allow yourself to get out of your own way and generate business by being of service to others.

# EVERY VILLAGE HAS A MARKETPLACE

It is said, "It takes a village to raise a child." We are all in this together, raising children, uplifting and supporting one another, earning our daily bread, and sharing common life-worries, sorrows, and more importantly, joys. From the Humblest Worker to the Highest Poo-bah of Success, we all have much the same needs, dreams, and ambitions. And we all have hard nights, when sleep does not come and doubts about our careers and our futures arise. That's all part of the life-curriculum of being a human being living on the spinning ball we call Planet Earth.

But every village has a marketplace, where we collectively bring our goods and services, where we barter and trade and create the synergy that forms the foundation of our economic lives. Marketplaces are full of ideas, energy, life and opportunity, but they are competitive by nature. At a marketplace, we don't always get what we want, or even need. We may even come away empty-handed one day. But we can always start anew tomorrow.

We're living in tough economic times these days. Unemployment and underemployment seem to be running rampant. Once-solid career trajectories suddenly stall or vanish. Long-term career stability often seems like a quaint idea from our country's Golden Era past. Even when we succeed, we still have a wary eye on the future: Can I buy that home? Start that business? Will I have a comfortable retirement? Am I doing enough? Is my bank balance big enough? How can I do more, have more, feel more in control of my financial destiny?

These common worries can cripple us. They can limit our potentials and our ability to envision clear horizons. They can trap us in patterns of thought, expectation and fear that blind us to what we have to offer.

Your career does not have to feel like an obstacle course. Life is not a "rat race." And you are not what you do for a living. I'll show you how to find your balance, rechannel career and money fears, avoid common self-sabotage behaviors and bring your *heart* and *soul* into your work life.

## SUCCESS IS NOT ITS OWN SOLUTION

Whatever we are seeking in life – a Higher Power, family, career, a bigger and better Beanie Baby® collection – we all want to succeed with our dreams and ambitions. It is human nature to look to the stars, keep hope alive, and strive to better our lives.

But what is success, really? In our fast-paced, exciting, consumer-driven culture, success seems to equate with money, and with the status and goods that money can bring. But as many of us have wondered, "Is this all there is?" Is having enough money coming into the checking account a definition of our success?

And how much is enough, anyway? The more we earn, the more we seem to need to stay ahead and keep our financial ships afloat. Is having money to invest and generate income a sign of success? What happens when there is a financial crisis and those assets take a hit? Or even a big hit, as we've recently seen? Things are stabilizing in that area, but what if it happens again?

My background is in television, and in addition, I own a Media Consulting & Coaching Company, TVGuestpert.com, and Jacquie Jordan Inc. Publishing. (These endeavors are all geared toward supporting clients' media platforms; television appearances, for example, and businesses.) In all of these areas, success seems to be defined clearly, yet narrowly. How many bookings are enough? How many books, movie or TV deals define us as successful? Once you've been a guest on Oprah, where do you go from there?

But here's something I've noticed in the midst of our "celebrity–fascinated" culture: Even the rich and famous have success issues. Think of child stars who never make the leap to adult performers with steady careers, or the One-Hit Wonder musicians, or the gifted twenty-something actress who drops off the map when she is thirty-something because she is deemed "too old." Does their brief time in the center spotlight define them? Do their investment portfolios validate them as human beings? Of course not.

We are not what we do.

We are not what we have.

We are not our salaries or bank balances.

We are not what others tell us we can be.

Career development and dependable incomes that make our lives thrive *are* vitally important, but they are a *means* to life, not the end points or goals. And if most of us already know this, why do we still feel the need to define ourselves via money and success?

It's natural to take a look around and compare ourselves to those whose careers, accomplishments and material success strike our interest and inspire us. But the downside of this practice is that there is always someone else who seems to have more than we do. And for many of us, that comparison can make us feel diminished – lessened, somehow. And then we stress out about what we have and don't have yet, where we (think we) are going or not going, or how we will end up when we retire.

Have you ever had an image of losing everything and winding up on the street? Believe me, these catastrophic fantasies happen to confident and accomplished people all the time. They've even crossed my mind on occasion. Worries strike us when we are most vulnerable.

Deep down, we all know that life is actually not about money and success. It is about who we are, how we do things, how we interact with the world around us, what we take in and what we give back. We need to find our inner balance. We need to connect our hearts and souls to what we do, how we do it, and what we hope to accomplish. Positivity. Happiness. Joy. It's a sense of connection to the living-breathing world around us.

# PART I

# The Five Pitfalls

Now that we know a bit about Heartfelt Marketing,
and how we've come to be out of balance based on
our misguided ideas of success, it's time to
really dive into some of the knee-jerk fear reactions
that we experience every day. I call them The Five Pitfalls,
and they can wreak havoc on your heart and soul
as well as on your pocketbook.

# CHAPTER 3

# Sabotage, Money Terror, and the Dead Zone

## THOSE OLD GROOVES

To move forward with our visions and dreams, we have to know who we are and why we truly want what we are going after. But it seems that we often live in a state of perpetual motion. How in the world can we know if we are off course from our hearts and desires, if we don't stop long enough to look up, get our bearings, and see where we are actually standing?

Pitfalls happen when we dwell in the groove, the rut, and allow brain-rot. This lifestyle is going through the motions, day by day, just to get through. It's meaningless. And a coffeehouse on every other corner is the powerhouse that pushes us along. We're afraid that if we actually stop, our world will fall apart. Or, that we'll have a moment to realize how much we really hate the life we're leading. Or worse off, who am I if I stop moving, anyway?

If we stopped, we might hear the terror. The terror just below the surface, that's been screaming at us for years yet we've denied that voice. We may think that if we were to allow ourselves to feel the terror, a wrecking ball would demolish our lives.

We may also have to admit that, if we stopped even for a little while, we're afraid that we'd feel immensely dissatisfied. We might even have to acknowledge that we've been living in the Dead Zone (the realization of the things we need to release.)

# PITFALL 1. THE QUICKSAND

***When Gravity Doesn't Work for Me.*** For the longest time, I suffered from money terror. I am not alone in this. It was as if I lived in a space where I believed that, when I climbed out of bed, gravity would not be there for me. It might be there for everybody else. It might have been there yesterday. But it would not be there for me today.

What I really mean is that I had a deep-seated belief that money would not be there for me today. This insidious and irrational fear was paralyzing. I was constantly strategizing how to cope with the "What if . . . ?" and "How am I going to . . . ?" fears of my day and of my life. In spite of all this, I showed remarkable creativity and functioned very highly at what I was actually doing for a living.

I thought that all my issues were money issues, and if I just had more money, I would have fewer problems. This belief, of course, only made me work more furiously.

It always felt like it was never enough. Not just money, but not enough time, not enough free time, not enough oxygen to breathe in the air. Seriously, I had no ability to breathe below my chest. And if you had said to me "Just breath, relax . . . ," you might as well have been speaking Martian.

(Deep, relaxed breathing is abdominal breathing. Watch the breathing of a quiet, contented baby, and then practice it yourself. You'll feel the difference immediately.)

***Turning the Corner***. Eventually, I came to a life-changing realization. I realized that my real problem was spiritual bankruptcy. I was spiritually bankrupt, and my focus on money was just a symptom of the problem. What I have come to learn was that I actually suffered from deep security issues, both emotional and material. I felt that if I could master my control over money and have plenty of it, then I would feel safe in the world. By all external appearances, I was a smiling Golden Girl. No one would know of my inner turbulence.

Realizing that I was spiritually bankrupt was a new beginning for me. Since then, I have been able to create a healthy relationship to money and build businesses doing what I enjoy and providing service to others. The inner security that I experience expresses itself in my outer life as tremendous abundance that I am privileged to share with others.

You know how they say that things happen for a reason? When I look back on my life from this young-midway point, I can clearly see that a larger picture was unfolding, perfectly designed for me. Yet at times, in the thick of it, it was misery.

The brilliant tapestry of my current life shows that situations were brought forward to give me the training for later professional experiences. My life was being laid out by brilliant design so that my unique gifts could be offered to the world.

I consider myself lucky. I have a tremendous willingness and curiosity that propels me in life in spite of my fears. Also, I was given the opportunity to redefine success and the way I do business. Once I made these changes, I was rewarded with a welcome relief from the emotional pain and fear of my old viewpoint and methods.

***Lemons into Lemonade.*** How did these changes come about? For one thing, I had a business experience very early on in my professional life that shook the foundation of the way I did business. At the time, I didn't realize that something that felt like the worst possible occurrence could actually turn out to be an amazing gift to me. It shook me to the core and fundamentally shifted my perspective.

I was in my mid-20s, and I was working for a start-up cable news network in New York City. I had left an established, but otherwise similar, network because my salary was higher at the new place and my job title was more prestigious.

We were about six weeks into the production of the show. Everyone seemed pretty happy and excited about their jobs. I was engaged to be married and our first house, in New Jersey, was in escrow. Everything seemed idyllic.

Then I received a notice from my bank that I had bounced several checks. I was confused, as I never bounced checks, and I knew I had recently deposited my paycheck.

When I arrived at work the following day, it quickly became apparent that others had also received similar notifications from their banks. The water cooler gossip flourished. The CFO was confronted by most of the staff, and we were asked to give it a few days until the situation was handled. Like good soldiers, we kept showing up.

In the end, to paraphrase Gertrude Stein, "There was no 'there' there"! We got a big apology at the end of that workweek for the month's work we had already completed and for which we were not going to be paid. In short, there was never any true funding in place. Oops!

I was devastated. This is America! I was outraged. After all, I had been lured away from my previous job and had left behind "security" – a weekly paycheck and health insurance for the bride-to-be. I had never heard of such a thing!

I had a month's worth of bills that got paid out of a savings account. I had written checks against not one, but two paychecks that had ultimately bounced.

The doors were shut on the new network. Scared and scarred, I backed out of buying the house. It felt to me as if everything were built on a foundation of quicksand.

There were murmurings about suing, but even then I knew, "What's the point of suing someone who doesn't have any money?" I quickly chose to move on with my life instead.

Ironically, the cable news network that I had been lured away from – "the secure job"– closed its doors nine months later.

Life is a series of lessons. It is the only way to live. "The alchemy is turning lemons into lemonade" – so says my friend, filmmaker Anat Baron. If we don't, we get stuck with bitter lemons as our fare and the wrinkles of bitterness on our faces.

*Taking Stock.* If we want to take stock of our lives as they are today, we need to ask ourselves a few questions:

- Are we showing up (as opposed to backing down) for ourselves as best we can?
- Are we showing up for our loved ones?
- Are we focused on being a worker among workers in our vocations?

- Is our day-to-day job in alignment with our dreams?

The trick to living a Heartfelt Marketing life, and Allowing the Universe to be Your Business Partner, is to know where you are today. Check in with yourself. Yes, you can create it all, but first you have to be honest with yourself.


## PITFALL 2. THE DEAD ZONE

One of the things I learned from the rubber-paychecks experience was that, going forward, I would always work for myself, even when I was working for someone else. If I were going to work for someone else in the traditional sense, then I would consider that person my client. In other words, I incorporated internally.

I also rid myself of the delusion that anyone else is my Source of supply and paycheck. I realized that I had been raised on the sugar-water of belief that we grow up, go to school, get good grades, go to college, get a job, get married and live happily and healthily ever after. We collect a paycheck from a steady job until we retire and then we collect Social Security while knocking golf balls around.

At that point, I was done with that lie. I then had to figure out what my new truth was going to be. I refused to live in that ditch I call the Dead Zone, devoid of passion, risk and purpose.

# PITFALL 3. THE BLACK HOLE

*The Money Terrorist.* No amount of money in the bank can make us feel safe. I learned this when I was in Las Vegas with a billionaire television star on a $50,000 speaking engagement. On his way up to the podium, he handed me a crumpled-up receipt for reimbursement. It was for a bagel, and the amount on it was $2.99.

I am not sitting in judgment of him over his need to be reimbursed on a business trip. Rather, I'm saddened by the pain of his money terror that I saw in that moment.

I met with a media-consultant client who was in her mid-30s. She had been an accountant for a Fortune 500 company, and that had enabled her to retire at an early age by living off the interest from her investments. She was seeking my professional advice about how to create a creative business life for herself.

For all intents and purposes, she had attained financial freedom. Yet, she confessed to me that she was afraid to get a second cat as a companion for her first cat. She feared that the cost of the additional cat food would be unaffordable for her.

Although both these people had financial freedom, they were living in the Black Hole of Money Terrorism.

*Out of the Black Hole – Financial Freedom.* We recognize true financial freedom when we see it. Perhaps we see a gesture of generosity uncontaminated by fear, and we feel our hearts stirring.

I get my hair blown out at the salon next to my favorite

restaurant in Santa Monica, California, very early in the morning. Whenever I'm there, I see the restaurant's kitchen assistant, Miguel, place a handful of breakfast egg sandwiches on two different sidewalk benches for the homeless veterans who sleep on the street. Miguel buys the breakfast sandwiches on his way in to work every day, even though he makes the minimum wage. I have never seen him flinch in fear of his giving.

***Money Terrorism Self-Checklist.*** If you answer "Yes" to three or more of the following questions, you may be terrorizing yourself about money:

- Do you obsess or worry about money much of the time?
- Does your life feel out of control if you go below a certain amount of money in your bank account?
- Do you lose sleep over money concerns?
- Are you staying in a job, career or profession that is unsatisfying, just because it "pays well?"
- Are you staying in a job that you love but doesn't pay well, thinking that passion is enough?
- Do you put off your dreams because they seem "too expensive?"
- Whether realistic or not, do you fear that you could end up homeless?
- Do you buy the cheapest item when you know you could afford a better quality item?
- Do other peoples' money issues stress you out or cause you anxiety?
- Do you live in vagueness around money, not knowing how much you have, the amounts of your recurring expenses, or the amount of your debt?

- Do you avoid balancing your checkbook, afraid that the final balance "won't be enough?"
- Are you miserly toward yourself and others?
- Do you use money to control the affections of others?
- Do you believe that you'll start living your dreams when you have a certain amount of money?
- Do you wonder what your purpose is?

Stay tuned for Chapter 5: The Great Snag, where I'll cover the language of money and how money can be like an unbalanced relationship.

Money is not good or bad or evil. It just is. Disarming our inner money terrorist is one step toward running our businesses and our lives from a place of Heartfelt Marketing.


## PITFALL 4. DOWN THE RABBIT HOLE

*"But, but, but . . ."* Sometimes success and money are not the issues. Often, we over-commit ourselves, avoid opportunities and even undermine ourselves via our own egos. That's when we engage in the tiresome practice of Excuses and Cover-Ups:

- I forgot.
- I'm sick (when I'm not).
- I forgot my cell-phone.
- There was too much traffic.
- They were supposed to follow up.
- They didn't tell me (when they did or I should've asked.)

*Sabotage from the Top Down – A Client Story.* I have a full day scheduled, and sometimes that makes everything seem to happen at a fast pace. I pull into a street parking space in front of Starbucks®. In Los Angeles, this is like winning the Lotto®, because parking is always at a premium. I consider it a good omen for what is about to follow. Then I drop scores of quarters into the meter.

This Starbucks® has been carefully chosen for its proximity to myself, my client and a high-profile publisher from Beverly Hills. Let me qualify: This publisher is the former president of one of the nation's largest publishing houses. We're lucky to be getting some of his valuable time.

It is 2:00 p.m. My client has not arrived. It is then 2:05 p.m. My client is still not there. She continues to be absent as I begin to get a familiar sinking feeling, as if I am in the movie Ground-hog Day, reliving a single uncomfortable experience, over and over again . . .

Flashback: One week earlier, same place, same time. Same meeting with my client, the publisher and myself. I arrive, but alas, I fail to land the Lotto® parking space that will reward me one week hence. My client is not there. Nor is she there several minutes later. My phone rings . . .

"The Doctor is going to be late for the meeting," my client's front-office assistant informs me.

"How late?" I ask, not happy. "A half hour." She apologizes, like all good assistants do.

I get a familiar sinking feeling. I have watched this train wreck happen in the past, in slow motion, with one too many clients.

I say. "Where is she right now?"

She hasn't left Malibu yet. Reality check: At this time of day, that's at least an hour-and-a-half's drive. Enter the publisher . . .

Back to the present. It is exactly one week after the first failed meeting. Here are the two of us again, and here my client isn't. Deep down, I know how this is going to end. My client will not arrive for the meeting on time, or even close to it. She's a capable, successful woman. Why has she botched two important meetings that she desired?

*Self-sabotage.* The situation is all too familiar, across every industry and field of endeavor. People say they are ready for a new opportunity, but when opportunity comes a-knocking, they sabotage themselves as it arrives. Why do so many people fall victim to self-sabotage?

I have had diverse experiences as a television producer, media consultant, and the founder of TVGuestpert.com. This broad range of experience has enabled me to see success from many different angles in many different people. I've seen the up-and-comers, the one-hit wonders, the tried-and-true and the comeback kid. Having worked as a producer with some of the most famous people in television and film, I have noticed, time and again, that there is a certain mechanism at work. When an opportunity for success is presented, *not everyone has the courage to show up for it.* This process might sound absolutely counter-intuitive, but it is all too familiar.

With that said, I honestly asked myself, "Am I capable of self-sabotage in my own work life?" The answer was an occasional humble "Yes." That question led to others:

- What can be done about self-sabotage, AKA getting in your own way?
- How can we see it coming?
- Are people even aware that they are doing it, or is

self-sabotage one of those activities that live in our blind spot?

- What can be done to prevent it?
- How can you keep from "going down with the ship" when others around you are self-sabotaging?

Many people may be aware of their self-sabotaging behaviors but are unable to stop. Many others are not even aware of what they're doing, tending to rationalize their actions (or nonactions) and their failure. The blame game can also become seductive, as it draws our focus away from ourselves and on to others – like vomiting up a whole array of accusations and excuses.

One last thing: My twice-late client? She is not my client any longer. And she never did get her desired book deal. I'm responsible for the company I choose to keep. Our business policy is, "One time is an accident; the second time is a train wreck." Two strikes and you are out!

Getting in our own way of what we say we want is an endless rabbit hole. There are two ways to confront this malaise. One is to give yourself permission to say that maybe you don't really want it or that you are not ready for it today. The other is to take full responsibility for it and show up. Counseling, therapy, master-mind groups, support groups, and 12-Step Programs for money such as Business Debtors Anonymous, Debtors Anonymous, Work-a-holics Anonymous are useful in overcoming self-sabotage.

Getting out of our own way is the most obvious and yet most difficult maneuver to make. I can't begin to point out other people's wacky self-sabotaging behavior without looking at and learning from my own. After all, if you spot it, you got it.

# PITFALL 5. THE ABYSS

*Leggo My Ego! – The Anger/Blame Game.* It's not pretty when we are dumped on without cause because someone needs to find somebody else to blame, and we happen to be in the wrong place at the wrong time.

It had taken 18 months to set up this movie deal with a major studio and with an A-List celebrity attached to the project. It had also taken 4 years to build the business plan behind it. (But by Hollywood standards, that's the fast track.) It would probably be another 1½ years before it got made, and yet another year before it would hit the big screen. Then it would take 1 weekend to determine its success.

In Hollywood, I know that a deal is real when the Business Affairs office wants your lawyer's phone number. I ask my clients all the time, "Did Business Affairs call?" If they didn't, it's all . . . smack.

When Business Affairs finally did call, it took three weeks for my producing partner to negotiate our Executive Producer deals. When my producing partner called to tell me that the deal was closed, take a guess at my reaction. (Hint: Not normal!)

I was furious with her.

This is where self-sabotage thinking took me: "Are you kidding me? Here we are splitting legal fees for a Century City law firm at $550.00 an hour, and you don't have the common courtesy to include me in that call? Thanks, partner."

"Sybil" (from the movie) reared her ugly head in my head because I didn't say out loud what had flashed through my mind.

Some faint voice in the back of my head was trying to break

through the shouting in the front room of my mind, saying, "Hello? Hey, Jacquie, you just closed another movie deal with Owen Wilson attached." "You just closed a movie deal during the Writers' Strike." "Jacquie, you just closed a movie deal." These were whispers that I could only faintly hear above the clamor of my own inner insanity.

All I could hear in my head was the shouting of, "How inconsiderate of her!" And all I could see was that she did something that was unfair. Or shall I say, I could accuse her of doing something that I deemed unfair. But it really wasn't. It was just a story in my head – a fantasy, not reality. But we are so responsible for the stories we tell ourselves and project onto the world.

In my professional life, I have the amazing opportunity to be the rainmaker of opportunity for my clients' media ambitions. It's remarkably satisfying.

I've also been on the receiving end of my clients' self-sabotage in missed meetings with me or my staff. I've witnessed the incredible self-destruction that comes forth when the fear of success rears its ugly head in the anger/blame game.

As I witness it, people have a preconceived notion of what "it" should look like or feel like. The "it" is the opportunity. They will reject an opportunity as not being good enough or right. It reminds me of the children's tale, Goldilocks and the Three Bears. "This porridge is too hot." "This porridge is too cold." It's crazy-making behavior of the highest disorder. The self-sabotaging person is so focused on an imagined, predetermined outcome that there is no allowance for the process.

In the course of a year, we had four different clients get into car accidents on the way to their very first live television interviews on morning shows. That is no accident.

# IGNORANCE IS NOT BLISS

*There is a principle which is a bar against all informa-*
*tion, which is proof against all arguments and which*
*cannot fail to keep a man in everlasting ignorance —*
*that principle is contempt prior to investigation."*
*— Herbert Spence*

A woman who was a sculptor came to me for some professional wisdom. She had a chance to have her art pieces shown
on consignment in a prestigious corporate office center. The
arrangement had been made by the owner of a small art gallery.
The owner was willing to drop his own commission, as he was
so excited for my sculptor friend to have this opportunity.

As my friend went on to explain the opportunity to me, she
began to pick apart the art gallery owner. She had a list of irrel-
evant claims as to why the art gallery owner was not someone
she wanted to be in business with. She didn't like the way he
kept his gallery. She wasn't sure that he had the experience
needed to properly sell her art. She hadn't yet seen a formal,
written offer.

My response was, "So what is the problem? Can you sell
your paintings from your living room? No? Then, it's a "yes"
until you have evidence that it needs to be a "no," which you
won't know until the formal offer is made. In the meantime,
why not?"

The stories we create in our heads before the information is
in!

*Check your Ego at the Door.* Wouldn't it be great if we could give our ego (our self-importance), over to a cute hatcheck guy or gal? I personally would lose my ticket. That's a great fantasy, but here is a more realistic way to check your ego when it flares up.

Checklist for self-sabotage coming from the ego:
- Are you absolutely sure you are right?
- Are you absolutely sure you were wronged?
- Do you need to speak or act immediately?
- Do you feel misunderstood in the context?
- Do you feel edgy, irritable, or resistant?
- Do you feel tired, drained, or in need of a nap? (Resistance often shows up in the body as the need to sleep.)
- Are you running late?
- Are you procrastinating on important tasks or communications?
- Did you forget something (again)?

*Wearing blinders.* In my job, I listen to the goals of my clients. If they describe that they want Navy blue, we try to deliver Navy blue. Sometimes, however, teal blue is the opportunity available in this moment. And because we are the professionals with intimate knowledge of the landscape of our industry, I get to say with confidence, "I can tell you, Navy blue is not going to come in, and if we pass on teal blue, it will be a while before that opportunity comes up again."

Some people will only see Navy blue and can't expand to the possibility of teal blue. By turning down teal blue, they miss out on that color being the vehicle to bring in the Navy blue opportunity they were seeking. The complaint is usually worded to us as, "You don't understand me." For us, sadly, it's just another missed opportunity due to limited vision.

People get scared of the possibility of their own success. This is a fact of our human condition. Having this fear isn't the problem. Not recognizing it is. It takes almost as much energy to dismount into a contraction as it does to mount into an expansion. When people get scared of success, they blame other people for their feelings of being "out of control." Staying unsuccessful and feeling small can feel safe to us. It's not safe, but it can feel that way.

There is an absolute "self-destruct" that I witness in people when they get scared that someone is going to take their idea, their money, their property, or their opportunity. They begin to operate from a place of anger and blame, story-creating, and paranoia.

The antidote to this way of being is the affirmation of "Yes." You might lose. Someone might steal your idea. You might lose money. The opportunity might disappear.

And what I have to say is, "So what?" In Heartfelt Marketing, we don't cave in and desert ourselves. We say "Yes", because we are more creative than just one idea, one book, or one design. We have an abundance of ideas, and we live from a place that makes room for those ideas in this world. The full faith in this action truly allows for the Universe to step in and support us. An expansive thought allows for solutions. A contractive thought annihilates possibility.

In Heartfelt Marketing, allowing is not passive. Allowing, or allowance, is courage in the midst of the unfolding, courage gained by trusting that efforts, combined with the power of the Universe, will pay off.

# PART II

# Allowing the Universe to Become Your Business Partner

Now that we've identified the pitfalls and the old habits that
keep us confined to business styles that don't work for us,
we can start our foray into Heartfelt Marketing.
First, I humbly ask that you pull a few old sayings
out of your vocabulary:
"You can't teach an old dog new tricks"
and
"Old habits die hard."
Let's instead replace them with this:
*To understand the heart and mind of a person, look not at*
*what he has already achieved, but at what he aspires to.*
*–Kahlil Gibran*

Old habits can die very quickly by adapting some of the
practices in this next section. New tricks will come with ease
if you are willing to open your heart to yourself,
your goals and aspirations. Will you achieve perfection?
Certainly not. Life is never perfect.
These next pages will address Heartfelt Marketing,
but like any bumpy road of destiny, they will also go deeper
into those things that keep us stuck. I am with you on the
same path of continually opening my heart to my
business, my goals, and the wonderful people I come
into contact with on my journey.
It's a journey of self-love and certain imperfection.
It's time. Time to stop disowning yourself, but to
understand your heart, show up with it and come from
your greatest authenticity.

# CHAPTER 4

# Coming from our Heart, not from our Head

*Daily meaning is as important as daily bread,*
*and recognition as necessary as cash. When we work,*
*we are searching "for a sort of life rather than a*
*Monday through Friday sort of dying."*
*— Studs Terkel,* Working

## HEARTFELT MARKETING –
## FROM ON TOP TO MOVING ON

It's 2005, and I am feeling at the top of my television-producer game. I've received Emmy nominations so prestigious that they would lead an obituary, been invited to speak at media conventions, and worked with the biggest talents in talk TV. I now have a talk show running on two different cable networks featuring huge, heavyweight, power-player hosts in the movie and television industries. The hosts, in turn, sit down with A-List talent every week to chew the fat, kibitz and engage in spirited conversation about the business of the industry. We produced shows about the Oscar ceremonies, the Cannes Film Festival, and summer blockbusters. I always say that I got a film degree in the three years that I spent overseeing the day-to-day production of the show. I was also getting well paid for my producing skills.

While working on the two television shows, I had launched a media consulting firm a few years earlier that had morphed into a media development company run by political strategist, Darice Fisher. My loyalties and responsibilities were starting to conflict. I bought a house and took on a mortgage as a single woman business-owner in Los Angeles, California, fully aware that most women in the world don't get to have this opportunity.

After producing the 100th episode of the movie television show, which had Steven Spielberg as the guest for two back-to-back shows, it was time to move fully into my own company.

I was able to test my faith by stepping out of the false belief in an employer, providing the steady paycheck, as my Source. I quickly discovered, however, that the steady paycheck had certainly felt a lot better than the reality of not having one.

After the shock wore off – and I'm pretty fast on my feet that way – panic set in. My inner Money Terrorist burst out of the closet with a mighty roar, "WTF! I just signed a big mortgage, and now I have no certain steady income revenue stream!" The money terrorist screams louder in my head, "I'm doomed! I'll lose the house, lose my down payment, lose my reputation, and lose everything I've built and bought and paid for! I'll be homeless, I'll be sleeping on friends' couches...!"

I did manage to beat back my Money Terrorist on those last two panic notes. I came to realize that I have skills and talents to offer, and if I put them to use in being of professional service to others, I'll always be fine.

## WHEN YOUR INNER MONEY TERRORIST REARS ITS HEAD

First, identify the voice of the Money Terrorist. This is relatively easy. When you hear a worst-case scenario unfolding in your head, this is your inner Money Terrorist speaking. When you hear predictions that you will fail, this is . . . guess who? Your best defense against your inner Money Terrorist is to expose its shenanigans, then move forward. Quite simply, we are talking about . . .

## FAITH OVER FEAR

As I was producing the talk shows, I wrote a book called *Get on TV!* (Sourcebooks, 2006) This book taught aspiring television expert guests (Guestperts™) how to develop a media platform and maximize their radio and television bookings and media careers. As a television producer, I found it so frustrating to see great talent not having access to the golden gates of media audiences. It was equally frustrating to see those who did have this access not knowing how to parlay that exposure into a steady revenue stream. Ultimately, the solution to that frustration was turned into my company – TVGuestpert.com – that provides media development service packages to a variety of expert clients.

You may, at any moment, invoke your own heart. When you do, you will move from fear to faith. It happens in little moments; for example, when you decide to take those small but important actions for your business. Or the gestures can be grand ones, like starting a new business in line with your passions. In my case, I took my frustration and turned it into an opportunity to live in my passion by connecting Guestperts™ with various media platforms.

## TWO AMERICAN MYTHS

**Don't Let Your Heart get Hoodwinked.**

"Myth" is an interesting word. It has at least two well-known meanings and connotations:

Myth. 1: a popular belief or tradition that has grown up around something or someone; especially: one embodying the ideals and institutions of a society or segment of society. 2: an unfounded or false notion. – *Merriam-Webster Dictionary*

So a myth is both a great and inspirational belief that can embody the ideals of a society and a suspicious idea, an unfounded or false notion. Maybe it can be both at once.

For instance, the Horatio Alger Myth holds that anyone can be a success here in America, the land of opportunity. The American Myth of Individualism is founded on a similar, older idea, one that goes back to the founding of our nation. In this new nation made up of immigrants, we can escape the unpredictability of kings and rigid hierarchies. We can vote and create our own destinies. We can buy land, build homes, and start farms or businesses. This is a land of free individuals, not a mass of feudal peasants beholden to aristocratic landlords. The USA became a great nation because of the power of these two myths, which inspired people across generations, propelled our ancestors to cross oceans and borders to immigrate here, and spurred them on to build a better life. And they did. And here we are.

But every myth can have its downside. A myth is an idea; as such, it can be reached for, but it can also fall outside our grasp. Businesses fail. Disasters large and small rain down. Life happens, and life does not always work out the way we expected or wanted it to.

Put more simply, we've bought into the Myth of Success and the Myth of Money. Success does *not* change everything, and having more money (or a certain amount of money) does *not* solve all our problems. When we forget our hearts, our lives and our sense of inner-outer balance, we fall prey to the shadow side of our inspirational American Myths. True, these are the ideas that can inspire us to shoot for the moon. But if we embrace them without full consciousness, we may get hoodwinked into disillusionment, become dispirited, and find ourselves in our darkest hours.

Embracing Heartfelt Marketing, finding that sense of freedom, wholeness and balance, helps us to create our own personal business and life mythology that we can design, live in and thrive within.

## WE ARE NOT SLAVES TO "THE MAN"

Another belief that holds us back is that we work for "The Man." In fact, we can all work for ourselves, even when we work for an employer.

The day of the cubicle desk slave is coming to an end. Technology is making it possible to be mobile in our ideas, our creativity, our communication, and our commerce without diminishing quality of service. In fact, the mobility of technology has only enhanced our productivity, connection, and communication. In many instances, even the corporate giant is eliminating the cubicle desk-slave job. The folks that are the safest in the wave of this recession, in my opinion, are the business owners, the self-creators, and the entrepreneurs.

Never has there been a time when so many people had the possibility of starting up their own businesses to be fully self-supporting by their very own means. Never has there been a time where the mompreneurs have had an opportunity to launch lucrative at-home businesses while raising their children. For those of us who never have fit into the box, this is our time to step up! If you have the capital or marketable talent or skill set to start a business, this is your opportunity.

Remember however, that each of us is a worker amongst workers, whether we're sitting in a cubicle or sitting eight steps away from the baby's room. Every job we do, every task we complete, every sale we make, every deal we strike, is all taking us someplace along our career roadmaps. You may feel trapped by your job, but each day you go to work, that job is an opportunity to reinforce your skills, and that makes you stronger and more resilient. And if you keep that positive attitude, you will be ready to make a change to another job, a new career, or a fresh startup business, when you see the opportunity arise. We can be enslaved by our fears, our illusions, and our doubts – but not by "The Man." Free your mind and heart, and the rest will follow.

# CAUTION: THE MONEY TERRORIST
# WANTS RESCUED

Today I got a call from a colleague and friend who is a fellow television producer. A huge project he's been working on is about to air tomorrow afternoon.

He says, "I don't want to tell anybody about finishing the show because then they will think I'm looking for work."

I say, "Well, you *are* looking for work."

He says, "Yeah, but I don't really want anybody to know."

I ask, "Then how are you supposed to get your next job?" (I thought I was stating the obvious.)

"I hate this stuff," he says.

Newsflash: Nobody is coming to our rescue. Nobody. And even though we live in a liberal democracy, we really are responsible for creating our own stories and our own lives. And we owe it to ourselves to be self-supporting.

In order to come from our hearts and not our heads, we need to know when we are in our minds. Clue: We are usually in our heads when we are being held hostage by the Money Terrorist within. We often operate our businesses as if marketing activities were the same as asking people to come to our rescue. The Money Terrorist would like us to think that.

But Heartfelt Marketers know that they have skill sets to offer and that their services would benefit others. The Heartfelt Marketer is not asking for anything. The Heartfelt Marketer is offering and sharing information. It's the Money Terrorist who asks for approval, acceptance, and reassurance.

Heartfelt Marketers trust that if he or she receives a "no", then that business or client is not the right fit. Our inner Money

Terrorists take a "no" and turn it into a personal assault and proof that we shouldn't be doing business anyway.

When we truly want to turn our businesses and revenues around, we will arrest the Money Terrorist and advocate for the Heartfelt Marketer.

# CHAPTER 5

# The Great Money Snag

*To be full of things is to be empty of God.*
*To be empty of things is to be full of God.*
*— Meister Eckhart*

S omewhere along the line in this journey, I discovered that I had a very distorted relationship with money. In the present or at some point in the past, you too may have noticed this about yourself, and you may be working on healing it. For me, this translated as a distorted relationship with doing service.

The exchange of money is simply a transaction between two parties in a relationship. So when money is out of balance, ultimately what is out of sync is something that exists *within a relationship*. You may want or expect too much, or you may value yourself too little. The relationship is the key to the problem and the solutions, not the money exchange. These distorted perceptions around money, service and relationships make up The Great Money Snag.

So what is money, and how does it work?

## MONEY IS A RELATIONSHIP

Money is a relationship that can exist between two people or between a person and a company (such as an employer) or institution (such as a bank or insurance company). Money is the agreed upon exchange of value between two entities. If you don't value yourself appropriately, guess where you're going to end up in this dynamic?

The cliché goes like this: "Beggars can't be choosers." But that is only true if you, first of all, define yourself as a beggar (perhaps a dangerous frame of mind to get into). Then you have to accept that relationship between you (the "beggar" looking for a business deal or transaction) and the greater business entity that can buy from you, hire you, and generally put you on the map.

Beggars *can* be choosers: Just because you want or need a business relationship does not mean that you have no power. Your knowledge, career experience, creative specialties, product or business service are all aspects of power. You are entering into negotiations for a business relationship as a carefully selected candidate, not as someone randomly picked out of a crowd.

So choose to be there. Choose to acknowledge your skills and service abilities, or the value of your product, and approach the potential relationship from a balanced place of equality. The buyer and the seller (you) ultimately want the exact same thing: A positive, useful and profitable business transaction or relationship. Just because the buyer is Bill Gates, Oprah or a General Electric executive does not mean that you have to be a beggar scrounging for a crumb from the table of plenty. And if you don't make the other party into a Higher Power, you do not have to be a Lesser Power.

So what happens when the two parties aren't in agreement upon the rate of exchange for service or a product? You get to go elsewhere. We see this in business, marriage, divorce, taxes, and buying houses. Two parties must come to an agreement upon the terms of any given exchange. Your personal self-worth, self-value, and self-esteem play a large part in these occasions of give-and-take. Never sell yourself short.

## THE LANGUAGE OF MONEY

The Japanese language has many different words for different types of love. In English, we have only one word to describe love. Even though we talk about puppy love, romantic love, love at first sight, love of the game, and the love that makes the world go 'round – all are variations of the same word and concept.

Japanese has few words to describe money; however, English has many, with different connotations. We have currency, accountability, value, worth, fiscal, financial, buck, dollar, moolah, dough, greenbacks, singles, fivers, fins, tenners, dead presidents, not on my nickel, panhandle, put it on my tab, pass the hat, credit, debt, and on and on. As Heartfelt Marketers, it helps us to use the language of money in an emotionally connected way, the same way in which we as a culture use words to express ourselves about money.

After all, money in the form of currency is an object. It is neutral. It should have no more resonance than a rock. However, it's obvious that money is greatly emotionally charged. People kill themselves over money. People kill each other over money. It seems kind of crazy, if you step back for a moment. The language of money is full of meaning, connotations, and emotion. Our relationship to its perceived value is important to us as individuals and as a society.

## SO MANY BENEFITS

When I really stop and pinch myself, I realize that I am a woman living in the Western World in the City of Los Angeles. I have the freedom to own my own home and my own business. I can choose my relationships on a variety of levels, from personal to professional. Even in 2010, most women on this planet do not get to experience the freedoms – freedom of choice, participation and opinion – that I get to have, to relish. I must remember this every day. I also take serious account of the women who came before me, who did not have the freedoms that I get to experience, but who sacrificed and paved the way.

Why do I say this? Because in a situation like ours, where we have so many advantages compared to many in the world, there are no victims, there are only volunteers. This statement applies to the choices that many of us have on a daily basis. We get to choose what we want to eat, read, and watch on TV. However, I didn't always realize I had so many choices, nor did I take full responsibility for those choices. So how is it that someone who has had this much opportunity and success could have an inner Money Terrorist? One simple word: FEAR. It's sometimes said that "fear" is an acronym whose letters stand for "False Evidence Appearing Real." (Or, as it feels in the moment, "F— Everything and Run!")

## LOVE AND MONEY

Before the Middle Ages in Europe, marriage was simply a business transaction. Then the concept of romantic love was introduced, as heard in the poems and songs of French trouba-dours, Shakespeare's *Romeo and Juliet,* and others. Today, marriage involves both love and business aspects.

Maybe we can take a lesson from these facts – the lesson that our endeavors can be like a marriage of love and business. It is possible to love what we do for a living. Or perhaps we can say that the other way around: It is possible to make a living doing what we love.

We talked earlier about the language differences between cultures around concepts of love and money. We also have an enmeshment of love and money. That is, we have the love of money, and we have money for love.

We can see the beginnings of "money for love" when we look at history and see that daughters were essentially sold by their fathers or families to future husbands for money (the dowry). On the young woman's family's side of the street, the benefits of arranging a good marriage for her included aggrandizing the extended family's status and financial security.

When romance was added to the mix, confusion set in. Traces of this relational and financial exchange are still reflected in terms such as "Sugar Daddy" and "Arm Candy", referring to a wealthy husband who secures a younger good-looking wife.

When we find ourselves wanting to control and hoard money, that focus may be a way of preventing ourselves from feeling money terror; that is, our feelings around our emotional or material insecurity issues. As we become Heartfelt Marketers, we get right with ourselves, our relationship with money and our unique gifts. We come to a place where we can offer these gifts in service so that we can experience the free flow gift of giving these talents to the world in a co-creation with a Higher

Power. When we co-create, the Higher Power supplies the Grace and we supply the footwork. This allows us to serve ourselves and others for the highest good and to create self supporting sustainability.

# CHAPTER 6

# Money Insecurity

*And the day came when the risk it took to*
*remain tight inside the bud was more painful*
*than the risk it took to blossom.*

*— Anais Nin*

## MONEY TELLS A STORY

Under some circumstances, money can tell a story. You can become quite skilled in reading the story.

For example, saving the receipts for cash expenditures is a story. Some folks do this and periodically add up the receipts to find out where all their cash went. Those receipts from last week can tell us their story of last week – the places they visited, where they went first on a certain day, what they bought and ate, and so forth.

How you spend money can tell the story of your values – how you value your time, body, living space, loved ones, pets and more. When you are compiling your taxes, money tells the story of how you lived and the choices you made over the past year. The story of money can reveal a tremendous amount of information.

When people want to experience healing in their relationship with money, one standard tool that they use is tracking their expenses and income. This is done easily enough by keeping all records of income and outgo throughout the month, calculating the totals for each category (housing, food, etc.) and reading the story it tells. You will see where your life is in balance and where it is out of balance. You can tell when something is "off." For example, if you want to develop your business and "don't have the money for it," the story of your money may help you find when your money said, "bye-bye" or was spent on status symbols instead of serving the greater good. If information is power, then reading the story of our money or our numbers empowers us to make informed decisions.

While it's valuable to use this information to understand our own stories, we don't want to define ourselves through money and status. It never works.

*Question:* What amount of money is enough?

*Answer:* That is the wrong question to ask.

*Explanation:* Life is not about Money!

## MONEY SECURITY ISSUES

As stated earlier, it takes the same amount of effort and energy to create a contraction in your life as it does to move into an expansion. Think about it. It takes the same effort to move into a larger place as it does a smaller place.

Fear and excitement are the same energy. Fear is the projection of a negative outcome, and excitement is the projection of a positive outcome. That's why the effort to worry about your business is the same as the effort to create and take action in your business.

Many business owners worry about how to balance between spending funds on marketing, which is a forward-motion action, and spending funds on overhead expenses. Marketing efforts are not necessarily direct income-producing returns. In many cases, marketing efforts require time and patience before a payoff is seen.

Working with business owners, I get to see the imbalance of spending. We often work with people who are afraid to spend on marketing but want magical results. On the flip side, we witness business owners who spend recklessly on marketing efforts with unrealistic expectations, like someone diving from a height of ten feet into two feet of water.

Marketing efforts truly require a rooted approach to clarity in business dealings. It is here that it really helps to allow the Universe to be Your Business Partner. Marketing efforts are like planting seeds. It's impossible to know in advance how the crop will grow and which plant will bear fruit. Nurturing our efforts along requires legwork on our part, but the rain and sunshine are out of our hands.

# LACK CONSCIOUSNESS

***What It Is and What It Does.*** Lack-consciousness, sometimes called deprivation-consciousness, is the deeply rooted, foundational belief that there isn't enough to go around of what we need or want. When we are in the state of lack consciousness, we believe that we ourselves (and probably our family members) are lacking and in a deprived state. Lack consciousness seems to particularly involve the areas of time, money and love. These are the resources that appear to be in short supply when we are in the state of lack-consciousness. In fact, a popular affirmation that addresses this problem is, "There is enough time. There is enough money. And there is enough love."

One immediate consequence of lack consciousness is the belief that we need to do what we can to get all that we can as fast as we can. Or in the words of a beer commercial of a bygone day, "Grab for all the gusto you can get." This seems to be how we currently define success – a gobbling, greedy Pac-Man® mentality.

Lack consciousness is far more than just an individual head-trip. It is pervasive in our culture and in our society, from the top on down. We often imitate what we admire in the outside world, and often, our role models for success teach exactly the wrong lessons, lessons that lack balance.

Lack consciousness is also a collective mindset disease. In some subtle and not-so-subtle ways, at a very young age, we are taught to be consumers and worker bees, with the belief and assumption that others will provide for us: The Big Boss, the Government, or the Powers That Be.

We can blame the Democrats (or the Republicans). We can

blame religion. We can blame the Pilgrims or Christopher Columbus. We can blame the stock market. We can blame Mary's little lamb. But we've seen that the blame game does little except distract us from the opportunity to "weed the garden at home." The main thing for Heartfelt Marketers is to open up our awareness to lack consciousness within ourselves and show up for a healing process in which we can recover.

I know from my own experience that I was using money to try to buy love and material security, because on some level I felt I was lacking. "I don't have enough – enough money, enough security, enough stuff! But if I accumulate enough things, money, time, love, recognition and career collateral, then I will finally be safe in this world, safe on planet Earth, safe with people." I was expressing the false belief that things would fill the hole in my heart created by my subconscious sense of lack.

I somehow felt that if I could become highly accomplished and build financial security, then I would be in control. This distorted belief system is not exclusively mine. As a society, our lack consciousness supports this Gotta Get Ahead paradigm.

***Big Shot-ism.*** I would do things in my crazy behavior like help someone out with a car payment – which seems generous on the surface. Who wouldn't want a friend who could help with a car payment? If I could compensate for somebody and pick up the check, I felt like I was in control, and therefore I was safe. I had power and influence. This gesture covered but also fed the fear created by my inner Money Terrorist. It certainly did not put an end to that fear.

Behavior like this, sometimes called Big Shot-ism, does not make for good business. Neither does it make for good self-care, as it feeds our inner Money Terrorist without ever coming to grips with it.

I was trying to feel safe by controlling things, people, places, and situations with money to ease an anxiety I didn't even know I had. But true giving is about giving from a full cup instead of one that we believe is almost empty. Wrong-headed giving starts when we are little. A frustrated mother offers the toddler a piece of candy on the condition that he'll "be good'" Conditional giving is insidious and sometimes difficult to recognize, both for the giver and the recipient. In Big Shot-ism, we are giving conditionally to others because the payoff for us is the delusion of being in control and therefore safe.

*Security*. My lack consciousness was keeping me from my own goals and owning my own power and contribution to society. I was becoming bitter, angry and resentful at all these people who were asking me for favors, even when I had set up that relationship paradigm myself. It was *my* lie, a lie against myself. This lie of lack consciousness was keeping me from owning my divinely given gifts. It was keeping me from trusting that I was capable of being of service and creating an abundant, prosperous life and business of my heart's desire. It wasn't just about "making a living." It didn't occur to me that creating a business could be both emotionally and financially satisfying. When that news did get through to me, it was like a revelation.

If we're going to work for someone else, we need to be clear within ourselves why we are doing it. If it's because we have mortgage, children, and a college tuition coming up, and we need the health insurance, then we can own that decision and the choices that led to this opportunity. We can even be thankful for The Man.

And let me add, we are always working for someone. There is always a recipient and a giver in every business exchange – a client is just a different form of boss. However, in this book, we are most often speaking to the entrepreneur business owner and those who wish to become one.

# CHAPTER 7

# Energetic Tackiness

## "WHAT'S IN IT FOR ME?"

Ever get scared to sell? It's like the person on the other end of the deal can smell that fear a mile away before you even open your mouth. It's the thought of, "I really need them to buy this from me." And even if those words never leave the thought-balloon in your brain, the customer inevitably runs. Talk about the power of the invisible reeking. And who says thoughts don't travel? Fear in a sales situation has the same rotten smell that's evident when you go into a job interview and desperately need the job. Attachment to outcomes smells like decaying desperateness. I call it Energetic Tackiness.

Selling does come easy to many. Some folks can "sell ice to an Eskimo." However, we can also feel when a sale doesn't have heart. It's one thing to sell something and collect a paycheck; however, the stakes always feel higher when the authenticity of our hearts might be exposed. The payoff, beyond the financial, is that customers can feel a heart-sale over a head-sale.

## TACKY ON THE RECEIVING END

I get pitched ideas dozens of times per day. Most of them start out with lines like, "I've got the best . . . ," "It's the most . . . ," "It's never been done before . . . ," "I'm friends with . . . ," "You should be so impressed with . . . ." When the rotting baloney comes at you on a daily basis, it all starts to smell the same.

The nature of the game is for them to pitch me an idea that'll knock my socks off so that I'll create a show for them. Trust me, it's not an easy game for either side. Yet, it's painful to be on the receiving end when the pitch is a sham, either because the person selling it needs it desperately or doesn't actually believe in it, but wants me to buy into it anyway. Of course, none of this is ever said out loud or otherwise acknowledged. But the subtext of the whole dialogue floats around like toxic fumes in the atmosphere.

A call came in this morning from a young woman who says she has a big production company, knows the best friend of the President at Oprah Winfrey Network, and wants to sell a show with one of our clients. Her questions are: "What have I done for this client?" and "What can I do for her for the client?" I'm not even sure what she is asking, but she comes across as being very determined. And naturally, I would love to see my client succeed. However, the Energetic Tackiness that I was feeling from the phone call reeked more of subtle bullying than an inviting posy of collaboration.

Any problem initiating a sale absolutely lies with our thinking. It doesn't matter whether you're selling an idea, a service, or a product. What matters is the belief system behind it. Instead of making the sale about, "Oh my goodness, I need this so badly," the selling points should be truthful and emphasize value and service to the customer. And unless that is absolutely clear in your heart and in your mind, don't attempt a sell. Period. It's that simple.

## ATTACHING A STORY

Attaching a story to a potential client is also unwise, because it's a way of talking ourselves out of the sale in our heads. It's naming all of the (imagined) reasons that the client will say no. It's deserting ourselves before even doing the footwork. In the alchemy of a Heartfelt Marketing sale, you do the footwork, holding in your mind's eye the best possible outcome – the highest good for yourself, your client, and everyone. You simultaneously release all attachment to results, without creating any story or drama (that you have no evidence for) about why the sale will flop. And instead of attaching stories to our clients, we can use our discernment to glean valuable information about them that will help our sales, as the following account illustrates.

The number-one sales person for an in-pool automatic vacuum sold one at every home where he was permitted to showcase the equipment. While he was training a rookie at one potential buyer's home, the rookie was unable to close the deal. As they walked back to the car, the trainer said to the rookie, "Follow me." He walked back to the house and knocked on the door. The homeowner answered, both curious and dumbfounded at their audacity in coming back. The trainer said to the homeowner, "I have never taken one of these pool vacuums back with me after a demonstration. You are going to buy it. Here is why. You are a successful businessman. (Information discernment: Size of house and designer car in the driveway.) You obviously don't clean your pool. (Information discernment: People who are that busy being successful are also too busy to clean their own pools.) I know you have pool people who clean for you, but we know they only come by weekly, which leaves the pool only marginally clean on all the other days of the week, depending on the weather. With this pool vacuum, you will have a clean pool *every* day of the week for your children. (Information discernment: Basketball hoop in driveway.)" Needless to say, the number one salesperson closed the deal and didn't have to take the pool vacuum back with him, after all. Furthermore, the homeowner hired the number one salesman to work at his company.

In my previous book, *Get on TV! The Insider's Guide to Pitching the Producers and Promoting Yourself,* I mentioned that family and friends are not the best people to practice your pitch on, because they are already biased in your favor, regardless of their proclaimed "neutrality." As you do Heartfelt Marketing, expect that some deals will not close, but hold tightly to the truth of what you know about what you are selling. (I'm using the language of marketing and sales interchangeably here.) The art of closing deals is also partly in the grace of learning from the deals that *didn't* close.

Our resistance to using the telephone to reach out is like a smothering weight; sometimes it really does seem like a "10,000-pound phone." Making calls, reaching out, and selling your services can feel like "heavy lifting." Suddenly, cleaning out the cat box looks more enticing than making that next marketing call. The resistance to the process is exactly where the muscle needs to be exercised.

## EXPOSURE DOES NOT EQUAL EMBARRASSMENT

Another area of resistance that I've witnessed in entrepreneurs is the fear of exposure, even though exposure is exactly what their business needs. When the fear of exposure comes up in marketing, it's usually the fear of being criticized, of making a mistake, or of being misperceived, misunderstood, and devalued. The process of perception can get out of hand if you are tightly identified with your company. Letting go of this fear is much easier for folks who work in larger organizations, where they can hide in the herd. But for those of us who are entrepreneurs and who identify with our businesses, others' perceptions about our businesses can be hard to separate from our own perceptions about ourselves.

A few years ago, I was on the cover of Woman's World magazine. The photo shoot was an absolute blast: a professional hairstylist, makeup artist, and photographer; a wind fan in my face to blow back my hair; and bottled juice brought to me on the set with a straw. Then, the moment came when the results were out of my control. A panic attack set in for me. What would I look like on the cover? Would it hurt or help my career? I was having middle-of-the-night shame attacks, as if I had made a bad mistake. All this was going on while Oprah Winfrey was confronting James Frey on national television for lying about his book, *A Million Little Pieces.* I felt like *I* was falling into a million little pieces! "Who am I to be on the cover of a magazine?" I thought. Or maybe I would be exposed as a fraud. And all this was in honor of promoting my book, *Get on TV!* which is all about being seen! Love the irony of my life's unfolding . . .

I've witnessed this same fear from my clients when they are about to receive major exposure. There is an excitement about all the possibilities that lie in front of them. Then comes the panic attack over the fact that they're not in control of what happens once they are exposed.

I wondered, "What is this?!" How do you market your business, your message or idea if you are going to freak out in the 9th inning with the bases loaded? I mean, "Come on. Really?"

I soon realized what the fear was about for me. It was about other people's perceptions of us being out of our control. This is almost funny, because my entire career has been about controlling and creating branding, which sure has a lot to do with other people's perceptions. But the truth is that when you have put yourself out there, you have very little control over how you're going to be received.

Roseanne Barr grabbing her crotch at a baseball game was intended to be funny, in the context of her own sense of humor. She didn't anticipate that she would be criticized for her derogatory actions against an American institution.

In a Heartfelt Marketing exchange, we come from the heart with how we are and what we are putting out there, no matter what. We know that we will grow and change, but we trust that we can effectively create successful results with authenticity of being – without having to pretend to be something we aren't. It's a risk, but the payoff can be unimaginable.

A high-profile figure that comes right out and says, "You

are right. I am wrong. I am guilty," fares so much better than
the high-profile figure that doesn't say anything (or worse, de-
nies guilt) when caught red-handed. (Many of us remember Bill
Clinton's declaration, "I did not have sexual relations with that
woman.")

## TENSION

In every sale, a tension exists. It's the tension between the desire
to sell and the "What's in it for me?" stance of the buyer. Each
side is leveraging or holding out for its own need to be met.
Heartfelt Marketers must find the zero point, the balance point,
between these two places. This must be done while keeping in
mind the intrinsic value of their service or product and while
drawing the customer in with value. The polarity of these two
opposites must exist in order to create the "call to action" for
the buyer.

In our media work, we must create the value of a Guestpert,
talent, or media property as being "hot" or "on the cutting edge"
for the network. There would be no tension if we were to say,
"Come meet our run-of-the-mill expert." There would be no
draw. The studio's fear of losing the talent or concept to a com-
petitor motivates the studio's call to action.

## DEADLINES VS. ALLOWANCE LINES

Eternally optimistic career coach and TVGuestpert Dianne
Gubin believes that if something is not vital and important, it

will go away in time. In other words, she sees procrastination as a *good* thing in some cases. She further says that matters will resolve themselves, if allowed to. For instance, she had been trying to get around to going to the local photocopy shop to do some large-scale copy work that could not be done in-house at her company, but she kept putting it off. Eventually, the other firm's attorney called and announced that they did not need the material after all. Her company was saved many thousands of dollars.

Allowance lines allow the process to lead the action steps. Deadlines enforce outcomes that may or may not be in alignment with the process or with the information that the process reveals. Deadlines are important, however, because when they are backed up by the big picture, they keep the work on course.

Diane says that maturity and perspective go together. Having perspective allows us to see that not everything is critical. Some things take time and results don't always come in, or at least not in our time frame. Business cycles must be taken into consideration from a perspective of experience. In Heartfelt Marketing, we understand that deadlines are immovable, such as dates that bills are due. Allowance lines allow the creative process to unfold into opportunity.

# CHAPTER 8

# Your Roadmap

*Never think that you are worthless.*
*God has paid an enormous amount for you.*
*And the gifts just keep arriving.*
— Rumi

## INTEGRATING YOUR STREETS, BOULEVARDS AND FREEWAYS

I am finding great compassion for those of us who never quite fit into the structural box. Beyond the day-to-day challenges for such people, we now have a global recession and its consequences to deal with. This brings up an overwhelming sense of fear and helplessness. How am I going to make a living? How am I going to feed myself? Am I going to be homeless? What about my children?

Concurrently, we're experiencing an information Renaissance. Technology moves information faster than our minds. However, when ideas move faster than our external world constructs physically allow, we float in a void of uncertainty between the conceived and the existing. It's like having one foot in your past and one in your present and the future has not yet materialized. Many of us know how to thrive in this space in between, but the rest of us are too scared. And even for the wise, nothing makes this transition comfortable, leading to collective money terror.

I wrote earlier about my own personal money terror, but now we are experiencing collective money terror. Careers that have been a lifetime in the making are obsolete almost overnight. Who needs a telephone operator when you have voicemail? Just twenty years ago, you were a fool if you didn't have stock in Viacom's Blockbuster®. Now the gigantic industry has closed its doors. We've also lost Tower Records® and other legendary places of commerce.

In the midst of all this change, some of us are able to see beyond the veil – beyond the illusion of our currently constructed reality. We see the possibilities of a new world, a new way of living, a new way of being and a new way to participate in our world. Yet, while seeing the vision, our reality still has us bound to mortgages, bank charges, time schedule constraints, and daily routines that crowd the vision out and into the background. We may experience a sense of frustration and loss, wondering how to put the zillion pieces together between our current creation and the creation that we envision.

In business, it's common to have two jobs or income streams at once. What is happening between these two places is that you are relying on the reality that provides while creating the reality that *will* provide.

But the process often feels overwhelming.

## ROADMAP IT OUT – INCHES GAIN MILES

So what do we do? There can be no vision without fronting up to the daily basics of day-to-day living. Many visionaries have difficulty anchoring their ideas to reality. We see it all of the time with the "starving artist" mentality or archetype. I'm a television producer with a media development company, and I work with experts in getting their messages out into the media and creating the media businesses behind their platforms. In this position, I get to witness and coach the action steps for people between their conceptual idea and reality. The biggest tool when working with others for me is to understand their big picture vision. I don't care how big it is – "Cure world hunger" or "I want to be Oprah," I just need to know what it is.

## GOALS ARE ASSETS

Many people consider their full contribution has to be the devotion and service of Mother Theresa or Amma "the hugging saint." Service doesn't have to be sacrifice. If we are tapped into our talents, our gifts, our passion and purpose, our primary assets, we are then embodied with the contribution that we are designed to bring forward, no matter the arena: Wall Street, nursery school, Calcutta. Each will be an asset to the world.

## FINDING THE DESTINATION

When I'm working with clients to figure out what their goals are, I need to know two very different things. One is how they are making their living now, and the other is what they would be doing for a living if they had all of the money in the world. The discrepancy between the two answers often reveals how far off the client is from being in alignment with her or his heart's desire.

Once I get an understanding of the big picture (the vision), then we can backtrack the route that leads to this destination, breaking down the route into smaller pieces, like you do when you're going on a big trip. You start knowing two things: Where you're starting from and where you're going.

In planning your trip, you'll need to select a route, estimate your time of arrival, predict how many miles you'll want to drive each day, identify where you're going to sleep each night, and prepare for the trip itself. The latter involves planning what to bring, shopping for items you don't already have, packing everything up, bringing along snacks, bringing along in-car activities for the kids, and more. As you can see, the vision – the destination in our road map scenario – becomes the guiding principle for making the many choices and selecting the many items required to get from here to there.

The universe is definitely piloting the experience, because we never know when we might have to take a detour or slam on the brakes for a panic-stop. In any case, the legwork and the prep work for the trip begin with us.

For some of us, our lives are already filled to the brim with daily commitments, so it seems impossible to navigate towards a new vision. But this kind of road mapping can guide us through the traffic of everyday life and actually get us somewhere eventually. We need to break the journey down into steps as we would on a road trip. In the end, we find that many legs of the journey add up to arrival at our destination.

## THE BIG LITTLE CHOICE

From "not believing" that gravity would anchor me (AKA my money terror), I have learned to wake up every day with a commitment to choosing my attitude and my experience of this day. Is today going to be one of abject dread? Or is today going to be a day when curiosity and wonder abound?

Road mapping for me requires that I look at what needs to be completed today, this week and this month. What I think the day will be like when I wake up is never actually how the day unfolds. However, creating my intention for the day is like choosing a direction on the road map. I can see where I'm going, even if I do end up having to take detours.

It is also important for me to choose who I want to be in the experience of my day. Do I want to be a person that moves with joy and an open heart as I do my work, show up for my tasks, and hold space for other's visions? Or do I want to be a victim, a martyr, or a complainer if the day is rough?

The unfolding of the day is always a mystery, even with the most thoughtful intention at the beginning of the day. The allowance for this unfolding is as important as the plan itself. In the language of one spiritual viewpoint, the road map, with its directiveness, is the masculine principle, and the allowance for flow in the present moment is the feminine principle. When the two are working in harmony together and neither one dominates, we are living in balance.

We have these same choices every day. The big choice is to come from the place of serenity and believe in that anchoring gravity. The little choices are the decisions to recommit ourselves to the big choice in every moment, in every inch of the journey.

This gift of choice is not something that we need to be indoctrinated into or climb Mount Sinai (which I did in 2005) to access. It's just the decision to do so. And we can decide to choose differently, because that is yet another choice. When we own our power of choice, we truly own ourselves.

## STAFF AND SNAKE

The rod or the staff has represented authority, masculine or sun energy or linear thinking. The snake represents the shadow, death and rebirth, creation, or feminine energy.

(In it's simplicity, the shadow can refer to the dark or wounded side of our nature. Linear thinking refers to the thought process in which different elements lead logically along a "straight line" to a predictable outcome.)

We most commonly recognize both of these symbols combined as the trademark of the medical profession, but its metaphor reaches much further back. For purposes of our work, it's about combining linear thinking in balance with intuitive, receptive, and creative processes. It's the ability to possess both ideas and inspiration and to translate or anchor those ideas into our experience in three-dimensional reality.

As we know, all too often, some folks have great ideas, but they can't seem to pay their rent. Or the opposite, the dedicated, detail-oriented assistant, who is the backbone of the entire operation, can't see a bigger picture and never seeks or gets a promotion.

# THE FORWARD TRAJECTORY

*What Fuels the Rockets, Method or Madness?* I consider that there are two types of people. In the first group we have those who know what they want to do but, perhaps, don't know how to get there. Using the roadmap analogy, these people would be asking, "I know my destination, but what route do I take?" These folks are well-served, as we've seen, by breaking the road trip into a series of interim destinations on the way to the final destination. In practical terms, this process can be greatly aided by keeping pen and paper handy. If I get an idea, I write it down. At some point, I look at the components that make up the idea and I ask myself if these fit into the bigger picture of my vision.

The second group includes people who know what they want to do but might be going after it for all the wrong reasons. When we are moving toward creating the worlds, the lives, the businesses, we want to live, we are trying to anchor our visions to reality. Our motivation can be coming from either of two possible internal sources. One source is our "core wounding," that is, the unhealed, unrecovered wounds that we carry from earlier in life. The other, more positive possibility, is that we are co-creating our life along with a higher power, from a place of healing and recovery. This allows us to offer our vocation or calling in a way that can be of service to others.

I believe that up until the time I surrendered my life to a power greater than myself, I was living a life based on re-creating my core wounding, so my external life reflected my core wounding.

# ENVIRONMENTAL CRUSADER

A heavily credentialed environmental scholar was referred to my company to become a TVGuestpert. He is both brilliant and articulate, so we were thrilled at the prospect. He had been working on a book that had been no small task to design. It was a 700-page tome about how religious wars started the process of the environment's decimation. The book was very heavy reading but was also very effective. I would describe the book as a Molotov cocktail that would pull the security blanket off most people. While it was a killer topic in academic circles, it was also quite controversial. Those who took his stance knew the information already. Those who didn't back his position didn't want to know the information.

I knew this man had great dedication to his field. In order to understand his motivation – which I didn't believe was just to take on a 2,000-year-old religious belief – I asked, "What is your goal with this book?" He wanted to get across his idea that people who subscribe to religious belief systems often lack full understanding of how those beliefs impact global policy and the environment. The major religions of the world are not based on any scientific truth – it's like believing the world is still flat. This was his viewpoint. From our talks, his goal for the book was clear to me. Save the forests, streams, lakes, oceans and rivers. Proactive choice and responsibility, not following a flock of sheep.

Instead of picking a fight with historical facts, we launched a book that was based on present-day environmental challenges and explored how people could become part of the solution today and within the system that we are operating in. We culled several hundred articles and, in record time, put them all to-gether and completed a shorter book that places him on televi-sion shows as the expert who understands the present environmental challenges and how these will play out in the future, depending on the options we choose. He's become one of the leading speakers for young audiences on environmental topics.

His tome was published for those seeking to understand the deeper historical context of how global policy is made. This topic made sense as a second book.

So here we have two rockets being fueled. One is a blame rocket with a faulty guidance system and the other is a rocket with a well-tuned guidance system and programmed with clear instructions for how to reach the goal. A highroad, principled man, he, of course, chose the latter. His goal broadened and became an asset, not only to him, but to the world. Instead of putting people off, we were able to open up his message to many folks.

## IT'S IN YOUR HANDS

It's never easy to bring forth a solution for a vision coming out of core wounding. My purpose is to help clients avoid this by making them aware of the parts of ourselves that are blocking our success, which we may not otherwise recognize. I am not a psychologist. I do, however, believe that awareness and healing of our shadow, subconscious, wounded self is a life-long journey and is part of our evolution into maturity. It requires, first, ac-cepting parts of ourselves that are immature, undeveloped, wounded and scared. This acceptance is the first step on the journey of growth and positive change. On this journey, we become aware of chronic patterns of attitudes, emotions, and behaviors that are not in our own best interest. Part of the journey requires taking responsibility for these shadow parts of ourselves, even if they arose as a result of past non-optimal behavior of those around us. We need to take responsibility for them because we know they are ours now, and no-one else can do anything about them. These small gifts of insight are often our greatest antidotes to roadblocks, freeing us to bring forth our gifts. The unfolding of that process rests solely in the hands of each one of us.

I desire to live my life and to create a life with my Higher Power from the place of my healing, my conscious healing as opposed to my unconscious wounding. This is how I choose to live today to the best of my ability.

## WOUNDING AND MOTIVATIONAL CLARITY

We all develop our emotional dynamics in childhood when we model ourselves on and react to our primary caregivers. What makes childhood unique is that we enter life with a slate that's clean and devoid of pre-existing constructs of what reality and life are supposed to be. Over time, as we grow up, we draw conclusions about life and reality and develop our constructs about them through exposure to the teachings and reactions of those around us, our environment, and our own perceptions.

When we emancipate from our families of origin and strike out into the world as young adults, we tend to carry this childhood template along with us and continue to create our lives from the template. The inherent challenge in this situation is that these childhood templates often don't serve our adult life or our highest purpose and potential. Depending on the nature and depth of our wounding, we either re-create experiences in adult life that match those from our childhoods or we create the polar opposite in outward appearances and expressions to cover up the intended pain. One way or another, our inner woundedness stays the same, and in fact gets worse over time, until we enter a healing and recovery process.

Our childhood perceptions are often distorted, and even after the best of childhoods, we usually wind up absorbing some less-than-optimal relationship dynamics and emotional states and attitudes from our early experiences. When these dynamics begin to interfere with our emotional balance later in life, we must recognize them as our wounds. Coping skills that we developed to get through childhood may be out of date when we apply them as professional assets in adulthood. If we do not develop new coping skills, we chase people, places, things, and situations, always believing that the next one will be the one that fulfills us.

When we unleash our inner Money Terrorist, we are reacting from the wounds we suffered as kids. When we mature, some of us learn how to heal our emotional and money relationship dynamics, but most of us struggle, reacting to life and to our careers from a place of woundedness, not from a place of healing. And healing is all about achieving and maintaining that inner balance. It's about taking control and taking action, not about a life of knee-jerk reactions based on old patterns that operate automatically but do not truly serve us.

The irony here is that the balance point moves. So what used to work last year, last month, or yesterday may not work today. We need to be flexible and adjust to hold our inner balance point. It is the concept of homeostasis (always seeking a balance) in biology, but brought into the psychological realm.

What we need clarity on is our motivation about what we want from our career, business, our relationship with money, and life. To purposefully create lives from our core healing, we need to understand our motivations and seek balance. This is what will allow us to fully live and make choices. The passion of such a life is a sharp contrast to merely existing and feeling hemmed in, as we feel when we're living from our "core wounding," our default programming. Wounding motivation undermines our efforts and keeps us trapped in cycles of money terror or misaligned ambition. Healing, heartfelt motivation makes our efforts balanced and sound.

## THAT WONDERFUL GNAWING FEELING

If I have inside me a seed of a vision that wants to be birthed by and for me personally, it is impossible for me to stifle it. If I try to, it creates a gnawing feeling inside of me – a gnawing feeling that I'll call wonderful, because it marks the beginning of something new. I must create room in my life for the seed to express itself. If I don't and I ignore it, it dies, and a part of me dies also.

The flip side of the coin is that I often get ideas and downloads from my Higher Power that feel as if I must act on them immediately. What I have learned over time is that not every idea or inspiration is meant for me to act upon. I must learn to glean out what is important from my ideas and inspirations and to discern which of them will help me to craft my larger vision.

While working on my last book, *Get on TV! The Insider's Guide to Pitching the Producers and Promoting Yourself,* I was pitching a television show at a studio. The executive stopped me in my tracks and said, "Jacquie, I can't hear any more. The woman who just walked out of the room pitched a similar idea, and I already called Business Affairs." It was the first time I realized that ideas exist in the *zeitgeist.*

On the flip side, I've listened to hundreds of pitches, and pitches come in waves of ideas. Sometimes luck plays a part in who gets the idea into reality – sold as a television show, new fashion, or startup business. It's not necessarily based on the best credentials or the ability to bring the idea into reality. For me, the ideas that inspire action on my part are mostly the ones that come from the heart, and not the head.

## DAILY, WEEKLY, MONTHLY

### Daily Check-In List

- What do I need to do today to take care of myself? (Rest? Exercise? Nutrition? Meditation? Prayer? Play?)
- How much did I earn and spend today?
- What improvement can I make? Or what do I need to learn from this challenging circumstance or person?

**Weekly Check-In List**

- What goals do I need to accomplish – personally and professionally?

**Monthly Check-In List**

- Where do I need to land this month, financially?

Notice how each of these suggestions is devoid of the word "sale." Once the forcefully compulsive need to conquer and sell is released and replaced with moving toward our vision, we've begun to develop compassion toward our colleagues and ourselves.

## COMPASSION MONEY

*Compassionate Capitalism is Creative Capitalism.* In my company, when we earn or spend money, it feels good. We know we are earning from people who can afford us. We are not taking from others in a way that causes hardship. Our money relationships do not exist in a dominant/subordinate, parasitic, or vampiric way. We provide a high quality service with value that's customized for the client. When we pay employees, we pay them on time and at a fair wage. We believe in the investment of human capital. We work with high-quality vendors who are loyal and supportive of the vision of our company. In turn, we are also interested in supporting our vendor's visions. Knowing that our clients really can afford us, we do not retain late-paying clients. We do not keep on vendors or sub-contractors who are complainers, unhappy with their lives or jobs, or have poor attitudes. These are poisons that we cannot afford to have around our work. When we spend money on tax-consultation and other administrative expenses that are un-avoidable, we look deeply into the services that we are receiving, so that we do not taint our spending choices with Resentment.

Capitalism is by its nature creative. Build a better mousetrap, bring it to market and try to promote and sell it. But once the capitalist money-machine gets roaring along the economic road to profit, it can lose sight of itself. That's when we make unbalanced decisions based on need and/or greed. "I need to expand my client base and make more income, but I can't offer better quality service. So let the buyer beware. I am out for my own benefit." Or "Our shareholders are all-important, so let's freeze our employees' wages and cut their benefits to increase profits." This is the *opposite* of creativity. This approach actually decreases creative approaches to business and employee workflow.

Think about health-care insurance companies. They make record profits, yet they still hike up patients' premiums with no added benefit. Anthem® Blue Cross® did this recently, only to be met by massive customer outrage, not to mention a rebuke from the President and threat of legal action. And the irony of this Uncreative Capitalism is that the health-care companies are supposed to be helping us with our health care needs. But in reality, these are profit-making businesses and nothing more. They just happen to be selling health-care coverage. Insurance companies are paradoxical institutions. They fall under the con-struct of the collective agreement to buy into a way of living.

The question is – has this served us?

I call it Creative Capitalism when a business finds unique, service-added solutions to expand its bottom line or to expand or streamline its products and services. Creative Capitalism is not the sole domain of big companies. A delicatessen owner can practice it too. So can anyone who owns a business. The bottom line is this: Did you find your business only to rake in the income, or did you do it because you have something to offer your field, industry or customer base? Ask yourself: "Am I all about profit and money? Do I have narrow, bottom-line 'tunnel vision?' Or am I offering a service that is of benefit to another company or individual? Do I have passion and a heartfelt desire to do this work? Or is it something I fell into? Or is it a career that I worked hard to get into, but turned out to look better from the outside than from the inside?"

Doing business is vast frontier of possibilities, not a narrow gangway. By figuring out your personal and professional roadmap, sticking to it, and course-correcting periodically, you navigate that wide open space, and you can get to where you are going. Or you may even wind up in unexpected places, where new horizons, opportunities, and possibilities to expand your services live and thrive.

Navigating business horizons does require you to take stock of and understand exactly who you are, the first among several important questions.

**Who, What, Why and How?**

- Who are you?
- What are you trying to create?

- Why are you trying to do it?
- How can you be of service through the expression of your vocation and business?
- How can your business support you, your responsibilities, obligations, and goals?

These questions will help you synchronize your internal beliefs about who you are with what you are trying to create, why you are trying to do it, and how you can be of service through the expression of your vocation and business in a self-supporting, self-sustaining, and self-satisfying way.

# CHAPTER 9

# The Good, the Bad and the Ego

## THE EGO HAS LANDED

The word "ego" often has negative connotations. "She's egotistical." "My ego got in the way." "That experience hurt my ego." But ego is, in essence, a good thing, even a *great* thing. First, let's define the term:

> Ego is "the self especially as contrasted with another self or the world."
>
> – *Merriam-Webster Dictionary*

Hmm. So technically "ego" is a pretty neutral term, but we use it in contrast to egotism, which is an exaggerated sense of self, characterized by conceit, arrogance and self-importance.

Which begs the question, what is so wrong about feeling some sense of self-importance? Not a sense of ourselves above, beyond or superior to other people, but "self- importance" as a human being with an open heart, with something to offer personally and professionally.

To put yourself out into the marketplace requires ego.

Ego crossed oceans. It builds cities and skyscrapers, and it creates books and political movements. Ego got us to the moon and back. "I can do this!"

So a healthy sense of ego is not only fine and dandy, it's a necessary component of our personalities, as long as we keep it in perspective, in balance.

Interesting how that last word keeps popping up again and again. Balance is the key to so many things.

Know yourself. Respect your ego boundaries and the ego boundaries of others. Let your sense of self, your ego fly high, but stay grounded at the same time. Lose that balance, fly the ego too high, and it will come crashing back to earth like Icarus, from Greek mythology, who flew too close to the sun. Our dreams and aspirations power and drive our egos. So shoot for the moon, but stay connected to your heart in all things.

## THE BAD –
## AN ICARUS IMPERSONATOR

Years ago a very enthusiastic client of mine was about to embark on a new media career. This client was a leading expert in the field of beauty and longevity. It was a natural next phase to begin to share this client's vision and know-how with the world. Besides, the field was a hot topic, and I had no other Guestperts™ covering this area. It was a perfect partnership opportunity for both of us. Or so I thought.

Once this client got a little taste of what it was like to be on television, there was no stopping the juggernaut. Ordinarily I welcome such forward motion and drive. Although the client was passionate about the area, there seemed to be a very ego-centered mechanism at work. This was manifested by the client's second-guessing of all the recommendations from the wonderful team of established people whom I work with. I even found myself second-guessing my own judgment about the wisdom of slowing down the process and planning appearances strategically.

Through an outside contact, the client was fortunate enough to be asked to appear on Oprah. But the client didn't yet have the camera experience or the savvy to be at the top of the game on a show of such magnitude. The client also lacked the business infrastructure to support the after-effects of such a big media hit.

My client was not pleased by my lack of support, even though I could clearly see that an Oprah appearance was going to be too much, too soon, too fast. The client would hear none of my misgivings and was also unwilling to put forth the effort into meeting the opportunity, largely because of a sense of entitlement. The client jumped at the opportunity without much preparation. But after the show was taped, my client was cut out before the airing, never to be asked back.

## HEALING THE WOUND

We've already talked about how our money relationships can come from a place of imbalance and wounding. Now let's revisit the subject of turning wounding into healing.

Money terror is a delusion, as it is based in wounding

experiences and attitudes from our past. Finding that all-important inner balance is a big step toward letting go of our delusions and bringing forth clarity of vision and intent. When you get rid of those negative thoughts and doubts, you can see that reality is full of excitement, opportunity and the lively possibility of positive, creative change.

Money terror may create a crisis state: We lose our job, or our business flat-lines, or other external life-events may knock us forcefully from the path we have been following. So a career change or a new business may feel forced upon us.

It may hurt to feel shoved forward to considering new approaches, new options, and new opportunities. But instead of letting that hurt create a new wound, think of it this way. Wounds hurt initially. They can be painful and messy. But wounds do heal over and scar tissue is created. Scars may not be so nice to look at (but hey, they can be sexy, too!), but the scar tissue is tougher and stronger than what came before.

And scar tissue is also fresh new tissue that sits beside our original skin. Old realities meet new realities, as we shall see below.

## THE GOOD –
## WALKING BETWEEN THE WORLDS

Many creative people, including entrepreneurs and business owners, operate with one foot in the world that they know and one in the world that they're trying to create. When we met one of our early clients, Jonathan, he was a creative director at a prestigious advertising agency. It was perfect training for what

Jonathan was destined to become, the keyword being "creative."

At the time we got to know each other professionally, it was clear that Jonathan was bumping up against the constraints of a desk job and bursting at the seams to express his creativity. The universe offered up a creative outlet that Jonathan gladly accepted. He was asked to arrange flowers for an event – a small happening in his life, seemingly. Sometimes, opportunities can come right out of the blue.

With no experience, Jonathan jumped at the opportunity. In doing so, he discovered a wealth of untapped creative knowledge within himself. No wonder he was growing weary of his advertising job.

With one foot in his current world and the other in his emergent reality, Jonathan started working part-time and parlaying his creative design talents into other areas. He began experimenting and stretching his possibilities with every opportunity that came his way. He redecorated children's bedrooms, remodeled kitchens, and designed large-scale flower arrangements for parties, unfazed by his lack of formal training (other than having had a successful lifelong career in a creative profession). He eventually found his way to designing large-scale events.

## YES! GO FOR IT!

Then a seemingly serendipitous offer came his way. He was asked to appear on a television talk show about design. Like a baby who goes from crawling to walking on instinct, Jonathan began doing television appearances, and then he scored a three-book deal on his new passion.

And the universe does work: When it's ready for you to step fully into your newly created reality, it will collapse your pre-existing world as you knew it. The advertising agency that Jonathan had worked for folded. Jonathan was given a six-month severance package, which he utilized to complete his first book and launch his new business.

Today, Jonathan is an eclectic, highly regarded designer whose unique style can't be boxed in by labels. He is a national keynote speaker, a TVGuestpert, and a best-selling author of many books, sharing his creative genius with the world.

If you recognize yourself in any stage of this scenario, then congratulations! You are entering the same creative process.

It can be a bit schizy (schizoid) when you are between two worlds. I witness this with mothers whose children are about age five or six and they are reentering the workplace. With one foot in mommy land and one foot in the business world, they struggle like a caterpillar breaking out of a cocoon to establish a new footing in a new reality. Can you relate?

Sometimes you're thinking to yourself, "OK, when do I really get to be in the new world?" Then sometimes you're thinking, "I feel safer and more comfortable in the old world, thank you!"

One of the signs that you are in between vocations is when you are making money in one world and making tidbits of money in the new world. "Tidbits" means that the flow or stream of income from the new-world career hasn't become steady enough for you to make the full leap forward into the new world yet.

But receiving even tidbits of income from working at your passion is a promising sign. Keep at it, and your call to the universe will be answered. Too many times, I've seen friends and clients stop at this stage and fall back into their old world. Of course, this confirms their belief that the universe doesn't support their dreams.

Or you might find an interim form of work that points toward the new world. This is like using stepping-stones to cross a river. These are the jobs or professions that make us dribs and drabs of money and that may not be our final destination. But they do lead somewhere. You get to take a deep breath, recognize that the stepping-stones are leading you towards an as-yet unknown path, and keep putting one foot in front of the other.

## THE MOTHER OF INVENTION

"Necessity is the mother of invention." We've all heard that before, and no less a personage than Plato came up with it.

In Jonathan's story, "necessity" has two meanings. For one thing, Jonathan had reached the endpoint of his first career and needed a change. In addition, unbeknownst to him, his company was about to close its doors. The second meaning of the term, in Jonathan's case, flows from what the universe was throwing into his life path, a new opportunity to exercise his amazing talent for design. It was nothing Jonathan was expecting or had even been seeking. Opportunity sought *him* out. The change he made was a necessity for his survival and, simultaneously, a necessity for the care and nurturing of his creativity. The universe was working behind the scenes and presented him with a new roadmap for his career pathway.

Now you may not agree that the world works in such mysterious ways, but even the most hard-headed realist can see that opportunities do happen unexpectedly, and that by seizing the unexpected and running with that ball, new potentials do arise.

Life is an amazing dance between opportunity and action, and when it works out, this interaction seems inevitable somehow, as if it were meant to be. I do choose to see things that way. That's my experience of life: The universe, in my view, does provide. You just have to pay attention to the signals that lead to possibilities, and then have the courage and determination to go with that flow.

When necessity demands a life shift, when necessity provides novel new opportunities, you can become the mother of your own invention, or re-invention. Everyone likes stability, and we can be wary of what seems to be chance that takes us outside our habitual comfort zone.

But change is also dynamic and transformative. Keep an eye peeled when it arises and jump on any opportunity to create new pathways and revise your career roadmap.

Remember, if you've done your legwork all along, you will be able to recognize opportunity effortlessly and easily as it arrives, whereas before, you could not see it at all (possibly because you were too busy anxiously scanning your surroundings for Navy blue, when the opportunity was teal blue). Or you pushed back on the opening door because you were still plunging into your Pitfalls.

When you've been through the process of overcoming the Pitfalls and healing your inner Money Terrorist, you'll be able to live in the grace and ease of expansion rather than contraction. And "yes" will roll more easily off your tongue, because your inner compass is aligned with the direction that the Universe supports you in going. You will be practicing business from a Heartfelt Marketing place, and everything you do will attract chances to be of service to others and receive abundantly yourself.

# CHAPTER 10

# Rebooting Your Drive

Heartfelt Marketing is all about rebooting – just like rebooting a computer hard drive – restoring our drive to achieve success and deleting our misguided ambitions. It's about knowing clearly where and when we are starting out on our journeys and what goal each of us is seeking. But it's also a different way of understanding what is driving us. It's shifting from ambition to purpose and meaning. It's the ultimate reboot from Energetic Tackiness, Wounded Motivations and Money Terror to the serenity of being in the minute-to-minute slipstream of your life. That word – slipstream – has two meanings, both useful to us. The racing bicyclist who travels in the slipstream of air behind another racing bicyclist conserves strength because the second bicyclist requires less power to maintain speed. A slipstream is also when the main character of a fantasy story slips in and out of parallel realities. In the first slipstream, we save energy through teamwork. In the second, we are ready for anything life has to offer.

By now you're seeing that the heart of the matter is the reframing of goods and services. When our internal hard drive has been cleared of Pitfalls, wounded motivations and the tyrannical virus of the inner Money Terrorist, we can reframe the offerings of our business to be of service to others. In this state, we can truly bring forth the highest good for ourselves and others.

The "goods" part, as I like to define it, is Good Orderly Direction. It's a way of principle-based living. Not a perfectionistic way of living, but a foundation for running a business that chooses to function in integrity in a dog-eat-dog world.

Running a business on principles, such as service and integrity, takes courage. It's not always the softer, kinder, gentler way, but it's the sustainable way.

Running an operation from this perch will ruffle feathers. But you are not a conformist. You are not taking your place in line with a shuffling gait like those who plod along through life. You are taking more risks. You operate with less fear and more freedom.

Heartfelt Marketing, from a goods and services standpoint, creates a new business paradigm with new players. It is going to take risk-takers and leaders. It's going to take business owners who respect their own worth and value and; therefore, respect these in others. Heartfelt Marketing is not a fantasy-based operation. It encompasses the understanding that people will disagree and that things don't always turn out as planned. But for every disappointment comes a gift of something learned. And that gift is something to be passed on and shared.

The work of Heartfelt Marketing cannot be done in a vacuum. Sharing your experiences with others and forming partnerships, mastermind groups, and mentoring relationships with others will help to propagate the work of Heartfelt Marketing.

Imagine bookending a marketing call with a fellow Heartfelt Marketer. To bookend, you first identify a mentor, a trustworthy person who's on the same path that you are (in this case, the Heartfelt Marketing journey). You call this person before any important event; for example, before you embark on a marketing call. You discuss the important issues that you believe might come up during your important event. For example, on a marketing call, you might be concerned about engaging in Energetic Tackiness because sales have been slow recently. Having this conversation before making the marketing call releases you from the power that fear had over you and allows you to surrender yourself and the outcome of the marketing call to a power greater than yourself. Then you make the call. Then you call back the trusted-friend-who-shares-your-path and check in about how the marketing call went. You would discuss the outcome, the process you went through and what you felt and experienced. The two calls made to your trusted friend are the bookends, and the important event sandwiched between them is the call.

The key to running a successful business and having a successful life is to step out of the isolation of doing everything alone in favor of participating in community. When you are active in groups, business comes to you. It's the Law of Attraction versus the philosophy of chasing. Success happens in groups and in clusters. In fact when you look around at groups of successful people, you find out that many people know each other.

For example, the movie *American Graffiti* was directed by George Lucas. The cast featured Harrison Ford, Richard Dreyfus, Ron Howard, Suzanne Somers, Cindy Williams, and Mackenzie Phillips. At the time the movie was made, they were all unknowns except for Ron Howard who, of course, was known throughout America for his beloved character, Opie, on the long-running Andy Griffith Show from the 1960s. But all of them went on to become household names.

Though this example has been drawn from the entertainment industry, it is not unique to it. The value of breaking isolation, networking and having contacts in your business cannot be overestimated.

There is an exponential momentum when we are allied with others with whom we can hash out our ideas, be accountable for our actions and our progress, and share our victories. It's the simple principle of remembering that two heads are (sometimes way, way) better than one.

Not every day is going to be an A+ day of action and results. Sometimes it will feel like action is futile and does not yield results. So checking in with others is a good way to see where we are on the map of our lives and regain some perspective.

On the following page is a table of common problems in business and how they are handled using standard business solutions compared to Heartfelt Marketing solutions, with a note as to which chapter addresses the problem.

# HEARTFELT MARKETING TABLE

This guide to problem-solving can help you cope with daily challenges.

## BUSINESS VERSUS HEARTFELT MARKETING SOLUTIONS

| PROBLEM | BUSINESS SOLUTION | HEARTFELT MARKETING SOLUTION | SEE CHAPTER |
|---|---|---|---|
| Low sales | Work the phones | Reach out and begin conversations | 6, 10 |
| Slow receivables | Tighten billing terms | Identify customers who can pay and focus on serving them | 8 |
| Disorganization | Criticize employees | Examine your inner confusion | 3 |
| Workload | Crack the whip | Break it down, examine and fix | 8 |
| Disconnect from other businesses | Hire consultant | Create a support network | 10 |
| Message not reaching target | Advertise and promote | Identify the message and the target | 4, 8 |
| Delayed billings | Enforce calendar dates | Examine the payoff for delaying | 3 |
| Unproductive meetings | Success workshops | Bookend the meeting with a mentor | 10 |
| Deadlines out of control | Create Gantt charts | Identify deadlines that are real versus those that will go away by themselves without harm | 7 |

# AFTERWORD

As mentioned in the previous chapter, our Heartfelt Marketing journey is not done in a vacuum. First, it takes someone like you who is hungry for new information, new ways of doing business and new spiritual growth to get a book like this into the *zeitgeist*. I thank you from my heart for participating in my step-off into another chapter of my journey as I teeter on the edge of yet another phase of it. I fondly hope that this book's message is of service to others. That you took the time, energy and expense to come this far with me is a blessing.

Thank you.

– Jacquie Jordan

## *Alex Detail's Revolution*

### AN AMAZON BESTSELLER

Alex Detail has been kidnapped.

Again.

Ten years ago, Alex was a child genius who saved the world from The Harvesters, a mysterious alien force that attempted to extinguish Earth's sun.

A decade later, The Harvesters have returned, but Alex is no longer a prodigy and unwilling to fight another war. So someone at The House of Nations had him drugged and placed on the last remaining ARRAY warship, which is under heavy attack. Unfortunately for Alex's mysterious kidnappers (and the world) he has lost the mega IQ that allowed him to win the last war.

Now Alex must convince the ship's food-obsessed Captain Odessa to use his risky command program to save their ship, uncover his kidnapper's devious plot, and survive the war long enough to make it to Pluto, where, underneath the planet's frozen surface lies the only force in the universe that can stop The Harvesters.

### *Alex Detail's Rebellion*
#### THE SEQUEL TO
#### *Alex Detail's Revolution*

Alex Detail is being assassinated.

Again.

The second Harvester war has ended, but Alex has never been in greater peril. Not only is Alex being hunted by his deadly clone, the seven-year-old George Spell, he is also the target of a House of Nations plot to expose Alex's post-war experiments with The Harvesters and disgrace the genius war hero.

But when George Spell's latest attempt to assassinate Alex Detail at the New York planetarium nearly kills hundreds of people, Alex escapes death only to find his would-be assassin suddenly kidnapped by the powerful mystic, Brother Lonadoon.

Now Alex must join Captain Odessa on a covert interplanetary rescue operation where they uncover clues left thousands of years ago by an ancient race desperately trying to send a message to the future. But the message might be too late, as phenomena are revealing the beginnings of an extinction level event caused by the ongoing war between Alex Detail and George Spell, one that could lead to the destruction of the entire solar system.

BEYOND COSMIC DICE

Moral Life in a Random World

Jeff Schweitzer and Giuseppe Notarbartolo-di-Sciara

### *Beyond Cosmic Dice: Moral Life in a Random World*

by Dr. Jeff Schweitzer and Giuseppe Nortarbartolo-di-Sciara

*This is the book that ties it all together – the problems that religion creates in solving our looming problems, and the unholy environmental mess we're in. I'd say that someday we're going to have to listen to this man, but the truth is, that day is NOW.*

— Bill Maher

Morality is our biological destiny. We each have within us the awesome power to create our own meaning in life, our own sense of purpose, our own destiny. With a natural ethic we are able to move beyond the random hand of birth to pave our own road to a better life. Whereas religion claims that happiness is found from submission to a higher power, a natural ethic defines happiness as the freedom to discover within ourselves our inherent good, and then to act on that better instinct, not because of any mandate from above or in obedience to the Bible, but because we can. With the ability to choose to be good comes the obligation to make that choice; choosing to be moral is what makes us special as individuals and as a species. With a natural ethic we free ourselves from the arbitrary and destructive constraints of divine interference to create a path toward a full life for which we ourselves are responsible.

JACQUIEJORDANINCPUBLISHING.COM
TVGUESTPERT.COM

JEFF SCHWEITZER AND
GIUSEPPE NOTARBARTOLO-DI-SCIARA

## The New Moral Code

Also titled
*Beyond Cosmic Dice:*
*Moral Life in a Random World,*
with a new introduction.

by Dr. Jeff Schweitzer
and Giuseppe
Nortarbartolo-di-Sciara

In a confusing world in which faith no longer satisfies, *The New Moral Code* paves a clear path to happiness and fulfillment. The authors provide simple and easy steps to free you from the angst of today's modern society. Learn to shed the burden of expectation created by others and pave your own road to a meaningful life of deep contentment.

## FEATURED UPCOMING AUTHOR
## FOR JACQUIE JORDAN INC. PUBLISHING

For the enterprising 19-year-old Chelsea Krost, the word "entitlement" doesn't exist.

This diligent entrepreneurial teen is one of the hardest working kids in the nation . . . juggling roles as a radio talk show host, TV journalist, writer, motivational speaker, beauty product designer, teen philanthropist and college sophomore.

Chelsea is a much-sought-after resource on all topics related to the teenage experience and to the transition from teen to adult.

In March 2008, at just 17, Chelsea created the internet radio show "Teen Talk Live with Chelsea Krost," inspired by her own life experiences and everyday challenges as a teenager, Chelsea's goal was to provide other teens with a safe, non-judgmental outlet for sharing personal problems as well as global concerns.

Her message is: "Individuality is 'cool.' Don't be afraid to buck the trends and be yourself. Change begins with YOU."

2011 will be a banner year for Chelsea with the launch of her unique new "lip product line," the re-launch of her radio show and the celebration of the release of her upcoming book, published by Jacquie Jordan Inc.

## ADDITIONAL BOOK BY JACQUIE JORDAN

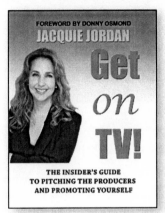

### Get on TV!
### The Insider's Guide to
### Pitching the Producers
### and Promoting Yourself

**Expert advice on
how to get booked
and asked back!**

"Jacquie ought to know how to
get you on TV . . . she's put half
the country on TV, including me."
– Maury Povich

In *Get on TV!*, Jacquie Jordan brings her expert advice straight to
you – the entrepreneurs, experts, authors, and future reality stars
looking to land a television spot. Jacquie shows you the ins and
outs of the TV business and what you need to do to get booked
(and asked back), including:

- The importance of tape and materials
- Speaking the language of the television producer
- Being persistent without being annoying
- What to do when you're booked and cancelled
- How to get asked back again and again

If you know the right moves, you can get on TV!

"Jacquie has the ability to maintain a fair balance between the
voice of the project she is producing and the needs of her
guests."
– John Edward, psychic medium
and author of *Crossing Over*,
host of John Edward: Cross
Country

Jacquie Jordan has been involved in booking, supervising or producing over 10,000 television guests, as well as coaching countless
people on how to get on air.

## HEARTFELT INVITATION TO PERU
## NEW YEAR

### Passion to Prosperity – Forgiveness
### to Freedom ~ Authenticity to Ecstasy

Join us on Machu Picchu on
New Year's Eve and New Year's Day,
for a Sacred Ceremony that will change the
very fabric of your life.

If you feel the call, have the opening to come, and trust our
amazing team to hold space for you – then let's just do it!

The architecture of many of our lives is under
going rapid reconstruction and unfolding, and
we are holding all thechanges in the highest regard
with the best possible outcome . . .
Journey with us to the Southern Heart of the planet to take
your endings and your beginnings to a new level of harmony,
surrender, wisdom and power.
This trip is designed so that you can participate at your own
pace. We will be staying at the exquisite sacred gardens of
W'ilka T'ika in beautiful comfortable surroundings – the perfect
retreat for having all your needs met – whether you want
time to yourself or desire the fellowship of the group.

Contact Jacquie Jordan, Richard Waner,
or Samantha Sweetwater
310 584-1504
Jacquie@heartfeltmarketingevents.com

**Jacquie Jordan** is the founder of Jacquie Jordan Inc./TVGuestpert.com, a media development, production and publishing company whose primary purpose is to raise the media profile of their Guestperts™ while developing the self supporting media businesses behind their brands.

Jacquie's foray in talent and production comes from her time in the trenches as a nationally recognized and Emmy nominated broadcast television producer.

Jacquie has been involved in booking, supervising or producing as many as 10,000+ television guests. Her reign has come from successfully launching and executing many syndicated daytime programs and cable shows.

She has been featured in *Entrepreneur Magazine, Selling Power Magazine, Feedback Magazine,* and on the cover of *Woman's World Magazine.* She is a television commentator regarding the business of the industry and pop culture. Jacquie's appearances include Fox Reality, Good Day New York, Fox, ABC Family, CBS, TV Guide Channel, ABC, FX and can be heard and seen weekly on News-Press Radio/KZSB 1290 AM Santa Barbara and Sony's Blip.TV.

Jacquie is the author of *Get on TV! The Insider's Guide to Pitching the Producers and Promoting Yourself!* (Sourcebooks 2006.) She will be leading a group of like-minded professionals through transformation from passion to prosperity in Machu Picchu this New Year's through HeartfeltMarketingEvents.com.

Breinigsville, PA USA
29 March 2011
258667BV00001B/8/P